The Curtain Lining Sketchbook

adapted by Wendy Baker for

Edmund Bell

Edmund Bell & Company Limited

Belfry House, Roydsdale Way,
Euroway Trading Estate,
Bradford BD4 6SU, UK
Tel: +44 (0) 1274 680000
Fax: +44 (0) 1274 680699
Email: sales@edmundbell.co.uk
Web: www.edmundbell.co.uk

The Curtain Lining Sketchbook

Wendy Baker

Introduction

Linings have many functions and benefits in the manufacture of soft furnishings and drapes. The primary function above all others is to protect face fabrics from the damage caused by ultra violet light. Severe deterioration can occur to fibre that does not have the protection afforded the dye ware used in the manufacture of linings.

Edmund Bell uses dyes that have been developed over many years. They have a high resistance to sunlight and prevent UV light from fading and causing deterioration of fibres. This protects expensive face fabrics and helps them to retain their visual qualities, giving them an extended life.

Sateen weave is used as the standard fabric construction because of the way it enhances the drape of the curtain and allows the fabric to be seen at its best. Cotton sateen is recognised as the best combination of fibre and weaving and can be processed to meet many requirements. This is the most popular type of lining.

When linings are used a barrier is created by the air trapped between the two layers of fabric, which in turn provides a thermal insulation benefit.

When interlining is also used there is an improved visual effect. The curtains have a rounder and fuller look, giving the impression of a higher priced and superior product. An added bonus is a noticeable increase in both thermal and sound insulation.

Blackout linings offer flexibility of sleeping times with the total exclusion of light. Additionally, they help to keep the heat out in the summer and in during the winter. Parents of young children, shift workers and hoteliers find these products irreplaceable. Our blackout linings have undergone rigorous testing to meet high demands of performance and aesthetic appeal.

When total exclusion of light is not necessary a dimout curtaining provides an attractive alternative.

Contents

Company History

The company was founded in 1855 by Edmund Bell, a merchant converter in textiles related entirely to the apparel trade.

Mr Bell was an astute businessman reputed to have made a fortune during the Franco-Prussian war (1870-75), selling fabric for uniforms. Edmund Bell had two sons Henry and Clifford who took over the business after he died in1890.

In 1906 a Mr Jenkinson and Mr Edwin Shepherd acquired the business. In 1937 Keith Runton was introduced to the company by Edgar Behrens, son of Sir Jacob Behrens and joined Bell's as Export Manager, much of the business being conducted abroad with countries such as Persia (Iran) and Australia. English textiles at this time were acknowledged as the finest quality anywhere in the world.

In 1939 on the death of Edwin Shepherd, Keith Runton bought the business and formed it into a limited company.

At the start of World War II, Bell's were still producing fabrics solely for the apparel trade and a large part of the business was making good quality cotton sateen dyed black for lining coats, suits and uniforms. This was known as Black Italian. The need soon arose for a fabric to black out every window in every house in the country to try to avoid giving help to the German bombers and a heavy Black Italian cloth was deemed ideal for this purpose. Bell's produced this throughout the war and unwittingly entered the domestic furnishing market as yet unaware that this was where their future lay.

In 1947 the company bought W.H.Childe and Son and moved into the premises in Chester Street, which were named Belfry House (this was used for many years as the brand name of Bell's) and remained here for nearly 50 years until it relocated to its present purpose-built premises in 1997.

The latter part of the 1950's saw Britain emerge from the period of austerity following the war when house refurbishment was becoming popular. This produced the demand for new curtains and the soft furnishing industry was reborn. A chance conversation between friends Keith Runton and Henry Armitage (owner of William Eyres, whose soft furnishing brand was Appletree Fabrics) resulted in a request that Bell's should dye Black Italian into lighter shades of beige for use in lining traditional domestic curtains.

Keith Runton was astute enough to realise that here was an opportunity to widen his range and increase sales in the growing soft furnishing market. At this time Bell's employed two travelling salesmen and a director who was based in the London office and looked after that area.

In 1961 Peter Runton, the younger son of Keith Runton joined the firm and with the two salesmen, Michael Birkett and Arthur Battye, continued to develop the soft furnishing side of linings. As with the original business they targeted the middle to top end of the trade and their reputation was founded on the best quality product and service. This reputation was to grow with the business for the next 15 years, as Edmund Bell became the market leaders in both quality and quantity. They still occupy this position today.

In the late 1960's another salesman was recruited - Dennis Noble whose background was in the textile finishing trade with Hunsworth Dyers and Naylor Jennings and whose job it was to develop business in the Greater London area. His appointment proved significant, as he was the best salesman the company ever had. His sales grew so substantially that at their peak he was responsible for a turnover of £3 million.

By the early 70's fashions in clothing were changing so fast that the traditional business was declining. In 1970 Peter Runton was made Sales Director and in 1971 Neil Williams was appointed as Managing Director. Together they channelled the company's energies into the Soft Furnishing industry so that sales of curtain linings soon became the core business for Edmund Bell. The mid 70's also saw the appointment of a Financial Director, Michael Boulton who was a qualified accountant and was responsible for the introduction of computerisation and management accounting.

The early 1980's saw the sales team grow and by 1984 there were six salesmen covering the whole country. This growth was reflected in sales, which had now grown to £4.5million. This compared to the 1930's when the company's turnover was in the region of £300,000 and 1961 when it was £750,000. All the growth was in Soft Furnishing products and by the end of the 80's the traditional clothing lining business had completely disappeared.

In 1988 Neil Williams retired, Keith Mitchell became Managing Director and the company saw considerable growth with the introduction of new products to reinforce the their position as the premier supplier of linings and allied products.

The 1990's saw an increase in turnover to more than £10million and an increase in the workforce from 18 to 34. Mr Mitchell left the company in 1999 and on December 15th 2000 the company was bought by Hanes Industries the textile division of Leggett and Platt an American multi-national company.

In 2005 Edmund Bell is celebrating its 150th anniversary. Turnover has increased significantly and the workforce now stands at 48. As the ultimate accolade, the company has just received the prestigious Queen's Award for Enterprise: International Trade 2005, becoming one of an elite group of companies to win the most coveted business award in the UK.

Edmund Bell is still the leading supplier of curtain linings in Europe, shipping more than 25 miles of fabric from the Bradford warehouse every working day. Today they are also a major supplier of face fabrics to the contract market for use in curtains, upholstery and other soft furnishings. It is their remarkable achievements in this area, which have landed them the Queen's Award.

Edmund Bell still has the same philosophy it had in 1855 – a total commitment to quality and service. 2005 is just the start of new chapter in the fascinating story of Edmund Bell & Co Ltd.

The Basics . . .

Curtain Headings

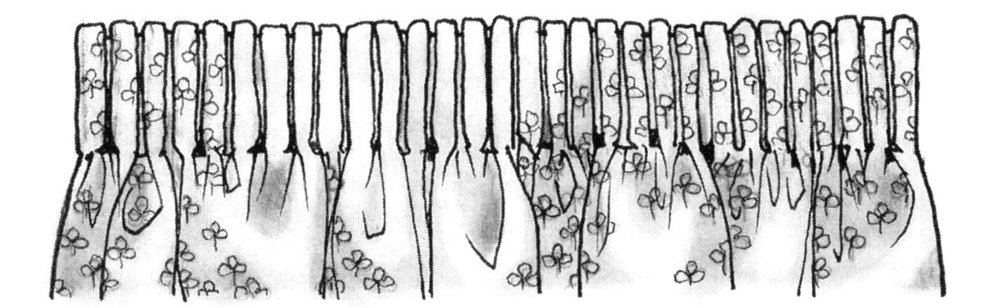

1

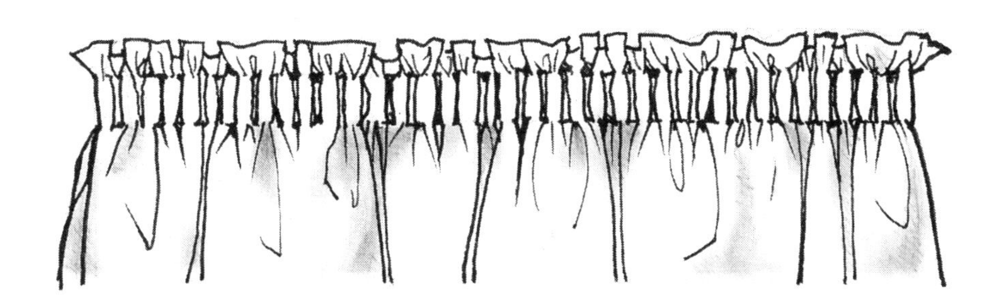

2

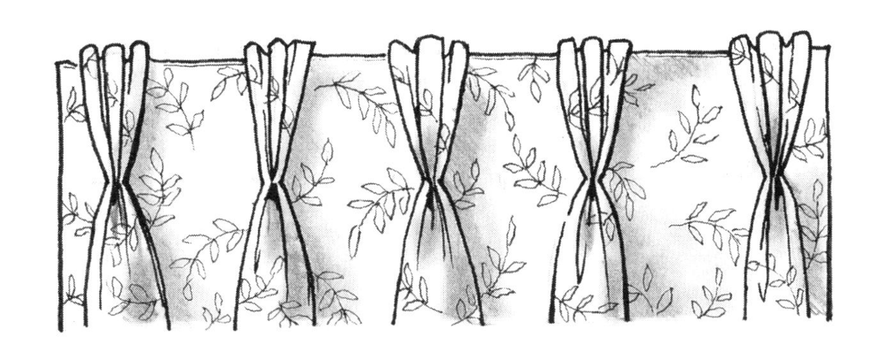

3

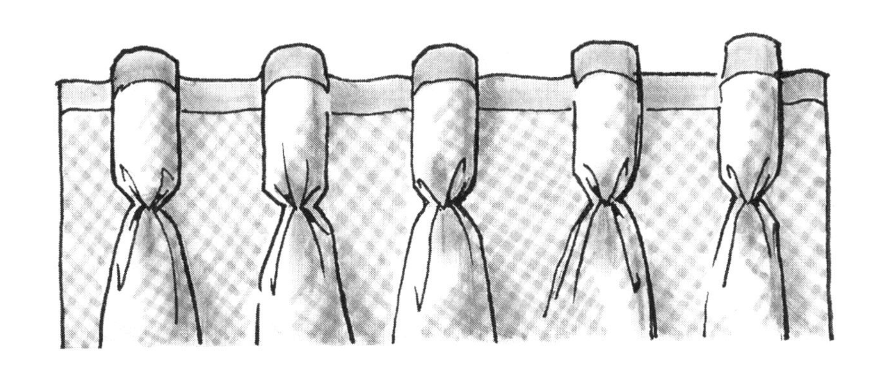

4

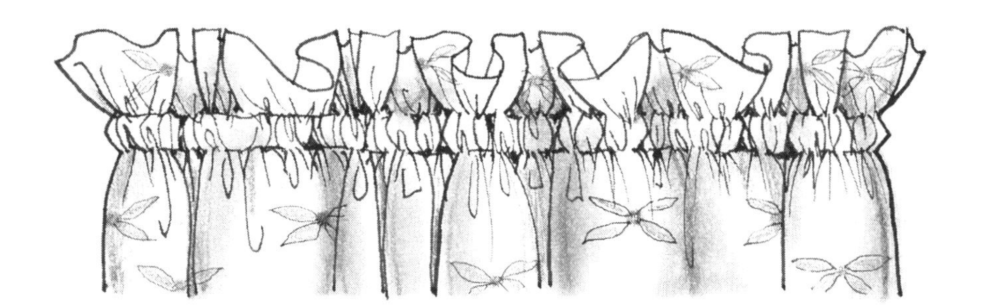

5

6

7

8

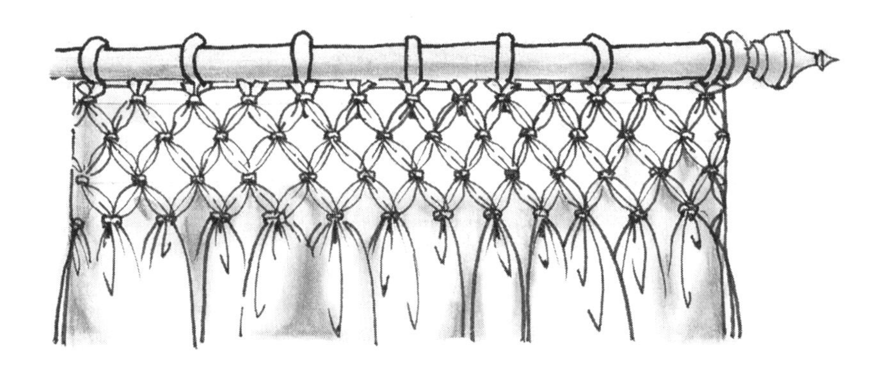

9

10

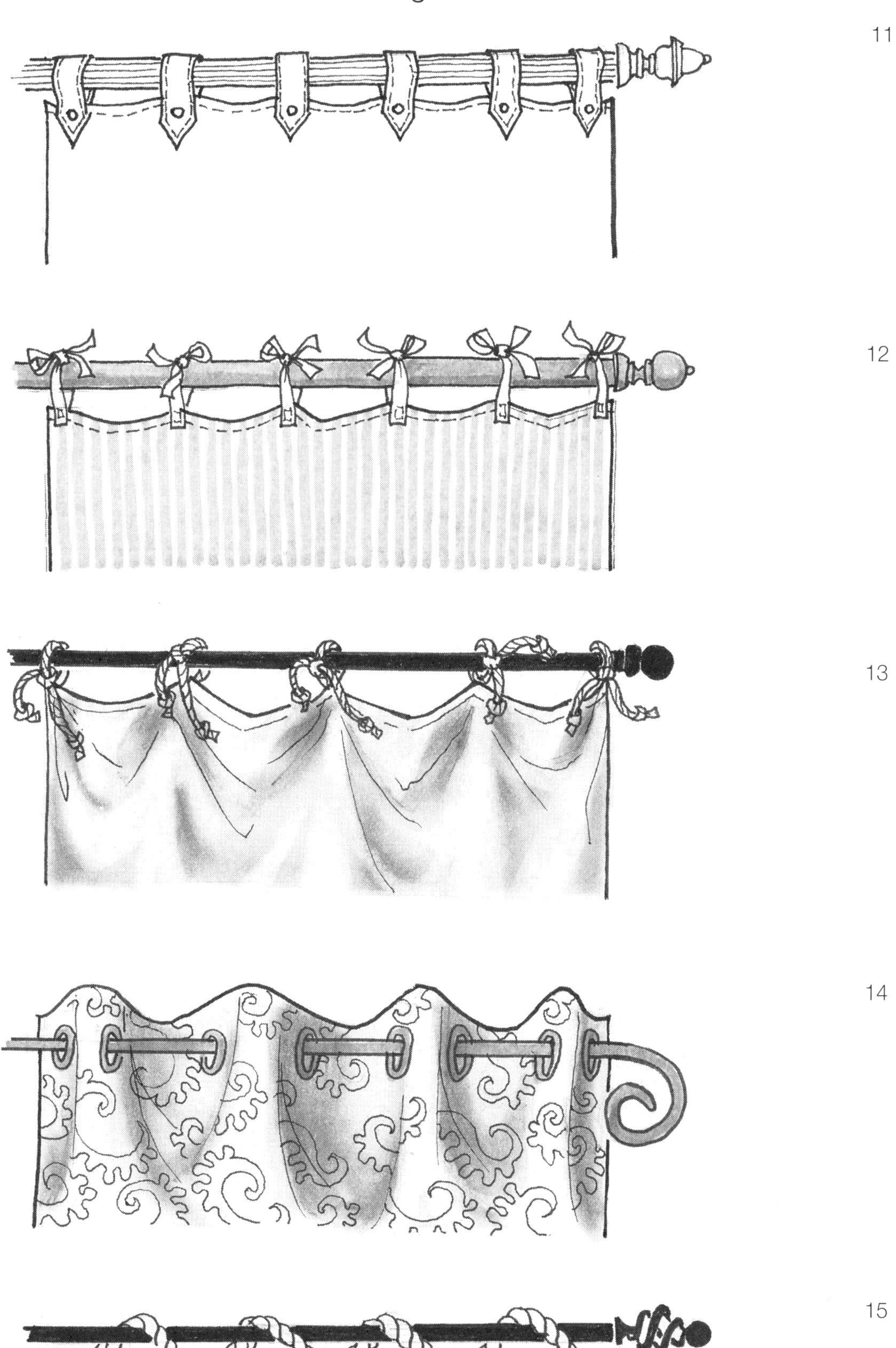
11
12
13
14
15

16

17

18

19

20

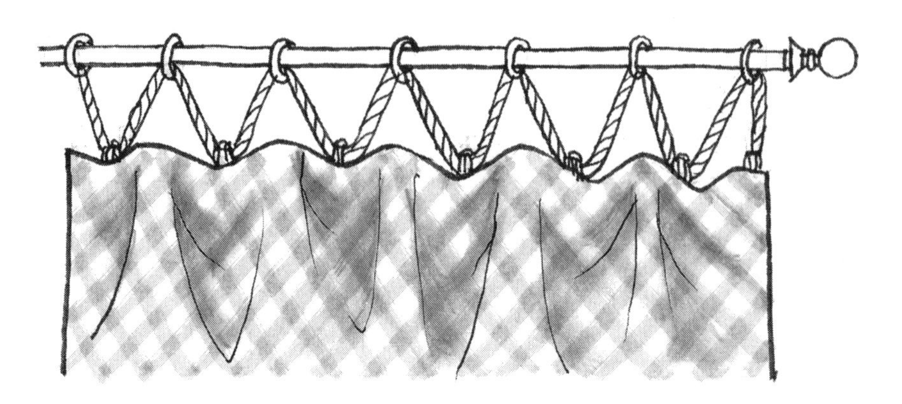

Valances and pelmets

I suggest using CHROMAX lining for the valances on the following pages – it is not expensive and it does give good protection against fading and rotting from sunlight.

Use DOMETTE to interline the valances as it is easy to use for all types of designs - however complicated they are.

For pelmet boards use DUO INTERLINING – the wadding goes under the top fabric to add a sumptuous finish.

Valances

1

2

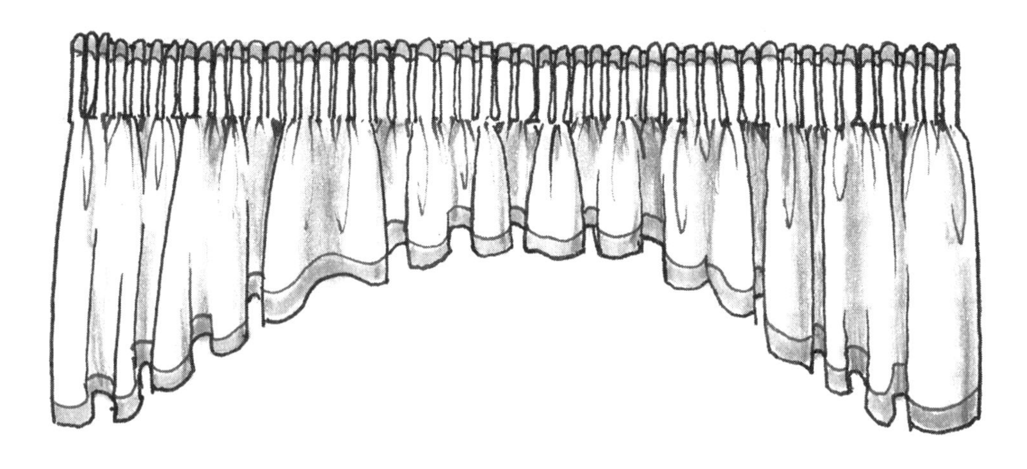

3

4

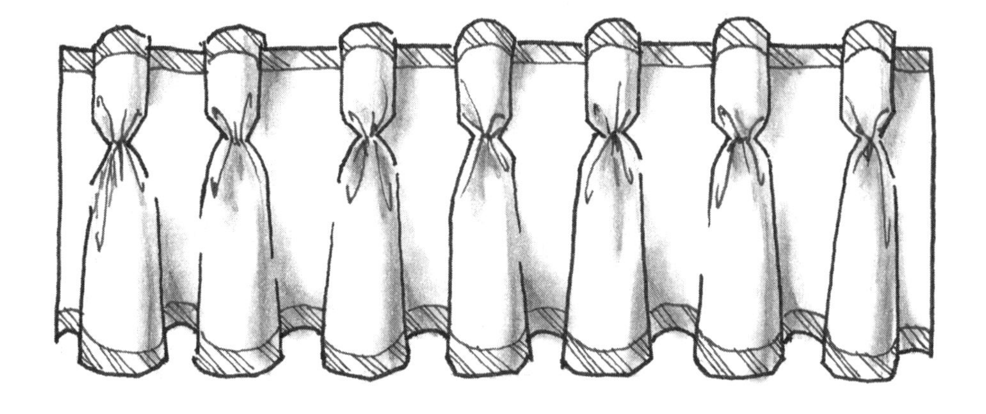

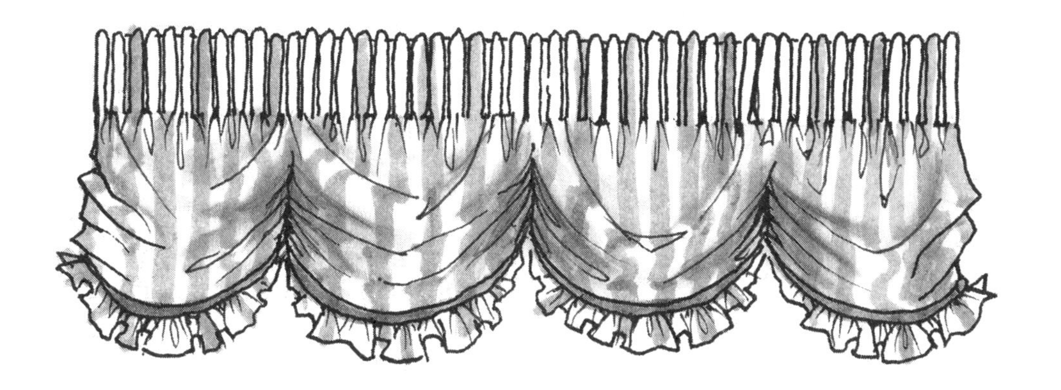

5

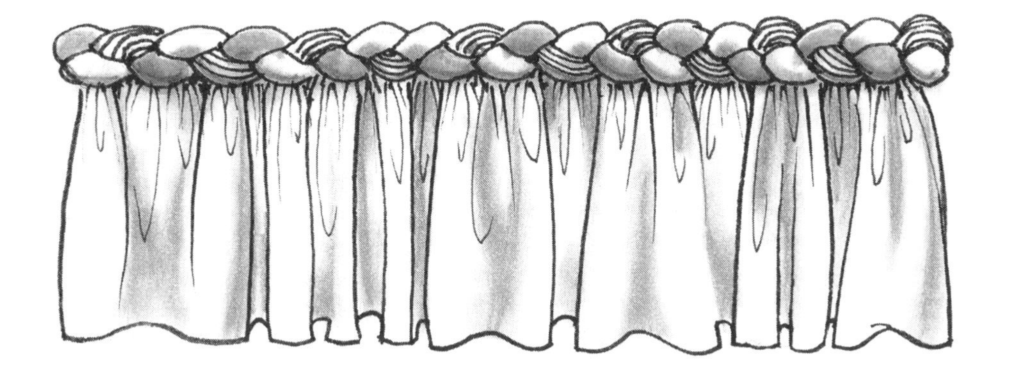

6

7

8

Pelmets

1

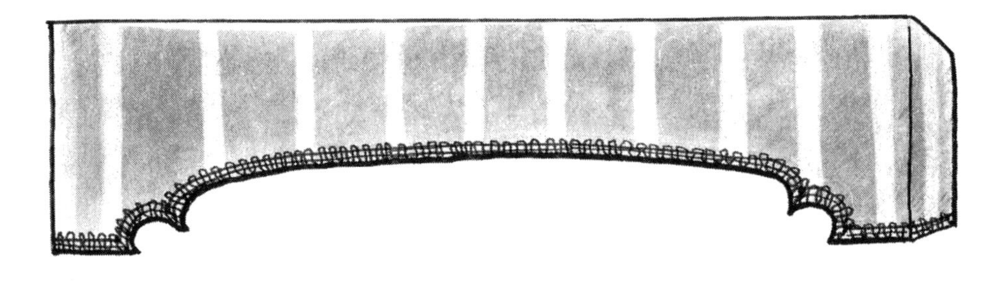

2

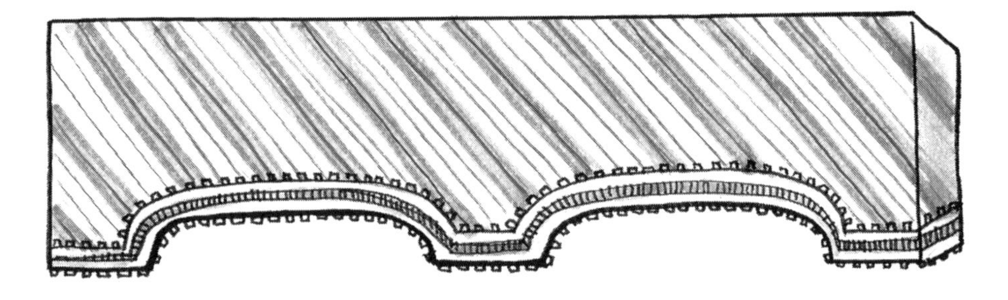

3

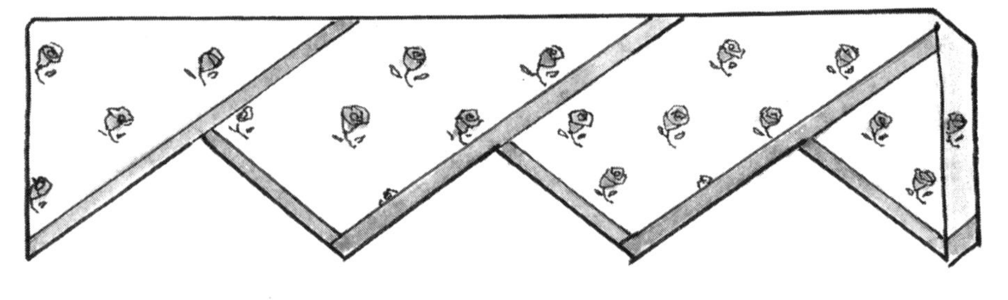

4

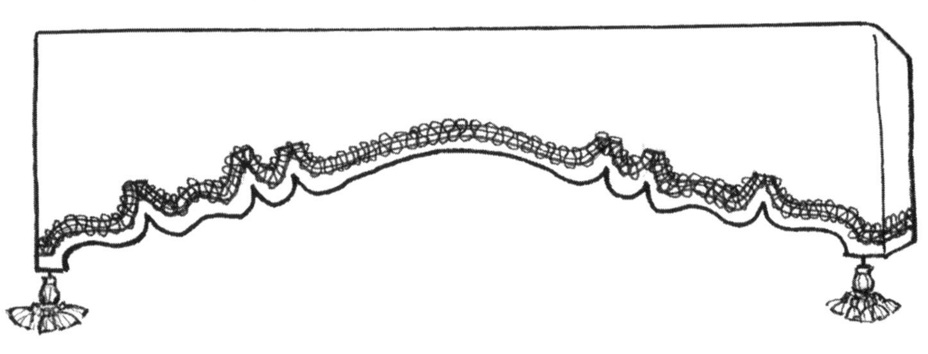

5

6

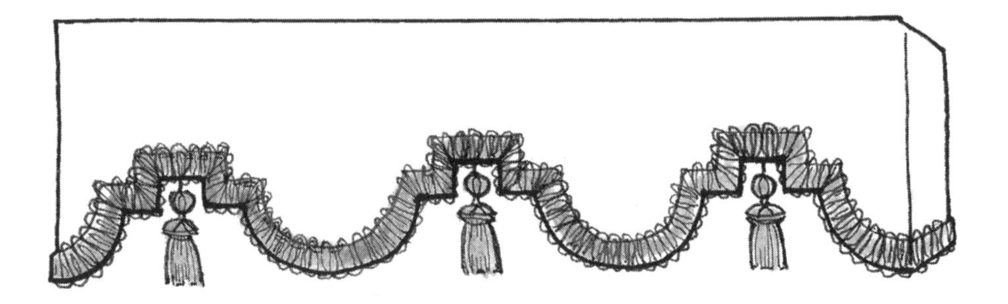

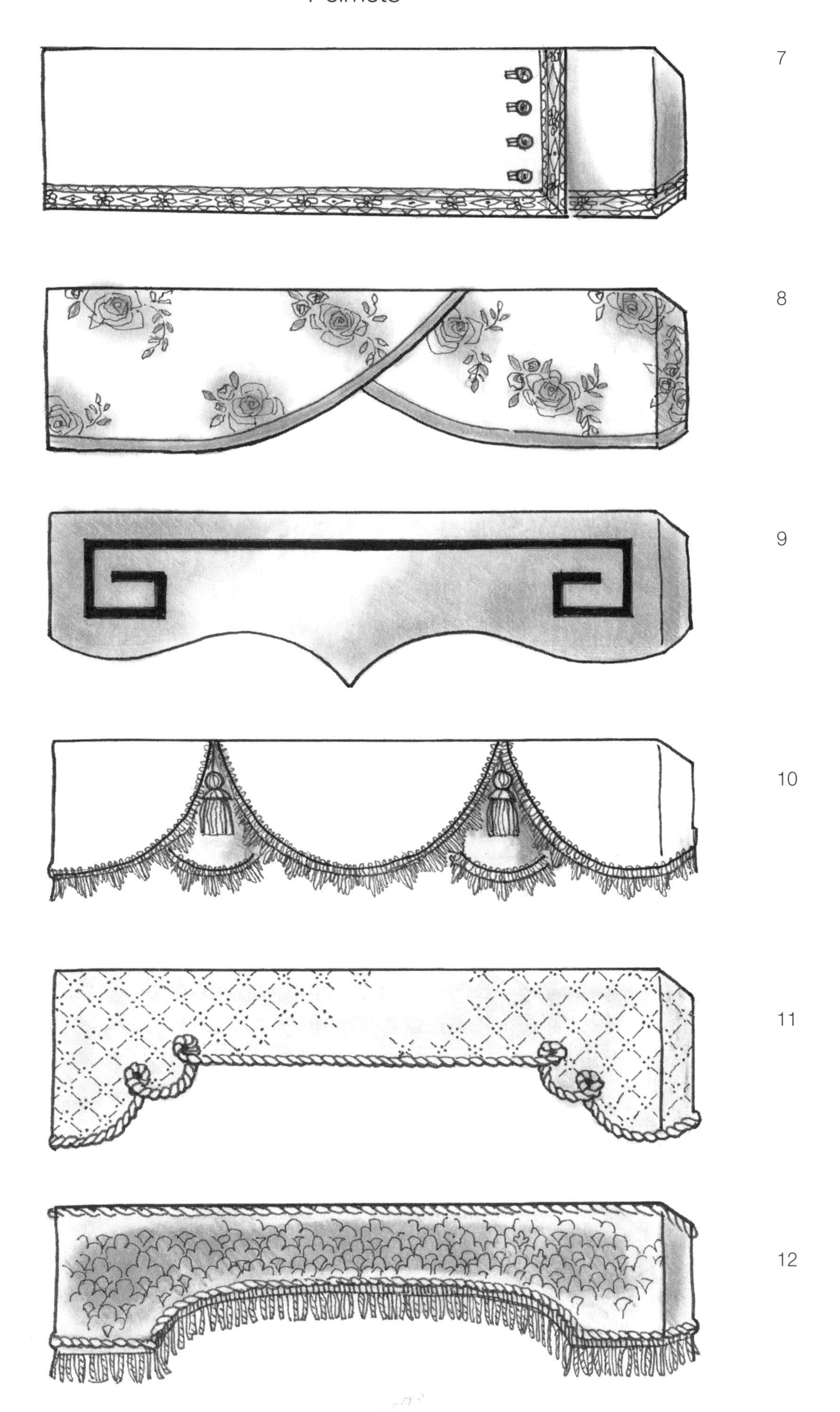
7
8
9
10
11
12

Tie Backs

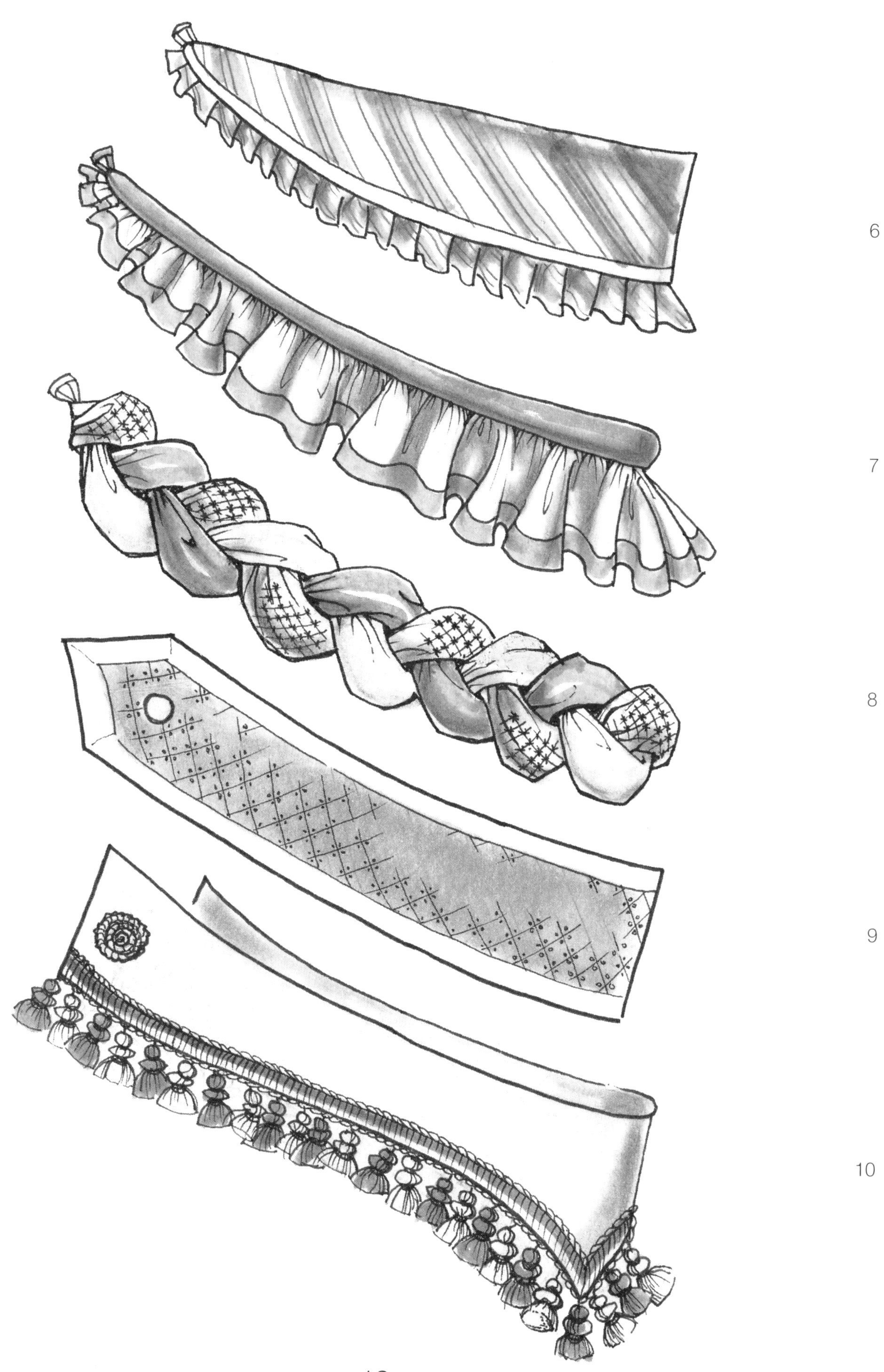
6
7
8
9
10

Curtains on poles

Here I would use CHROMASOL to line these basic curtains – it comes in neutral colours and is excellent quality for a sensible price.

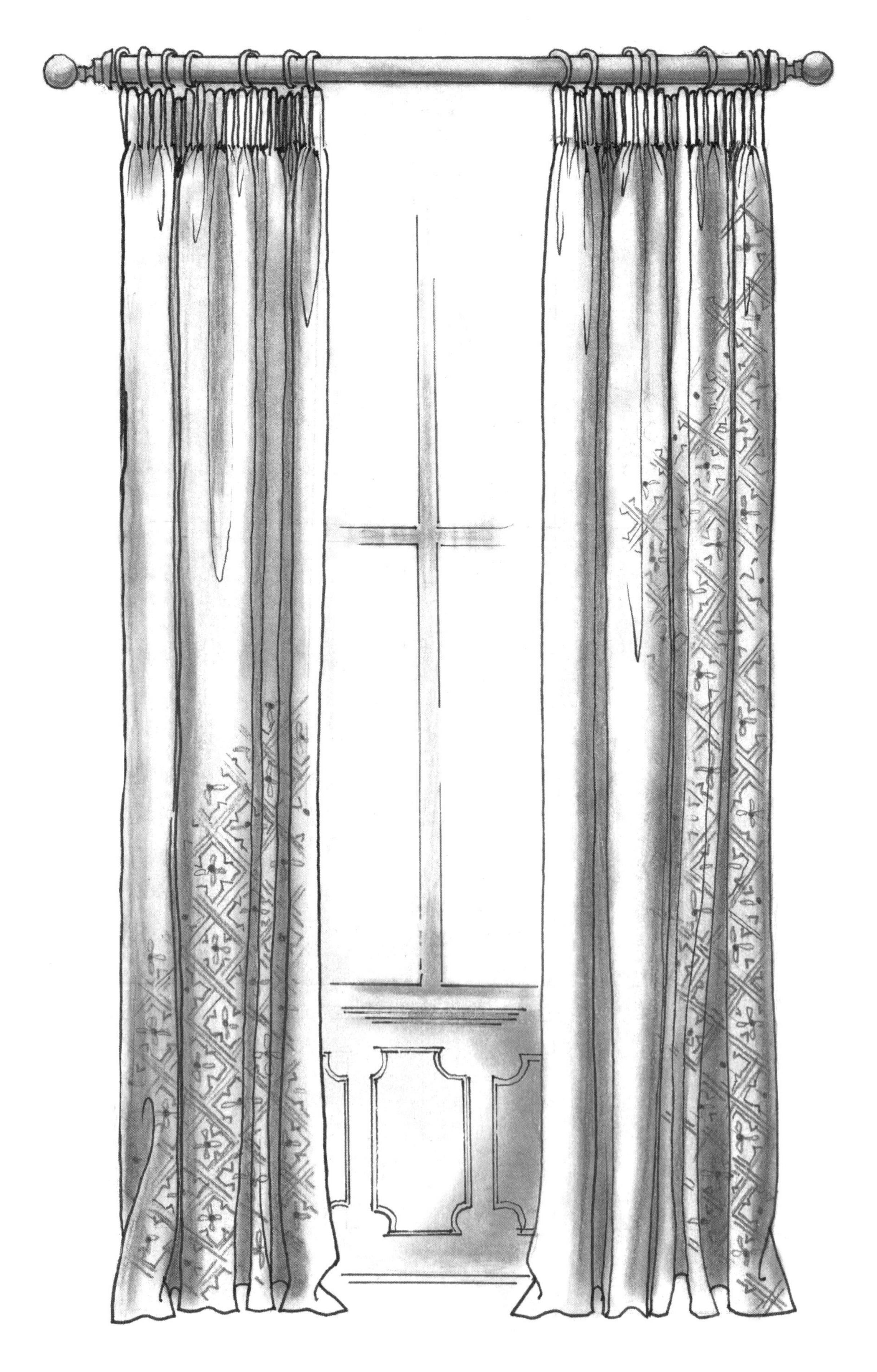

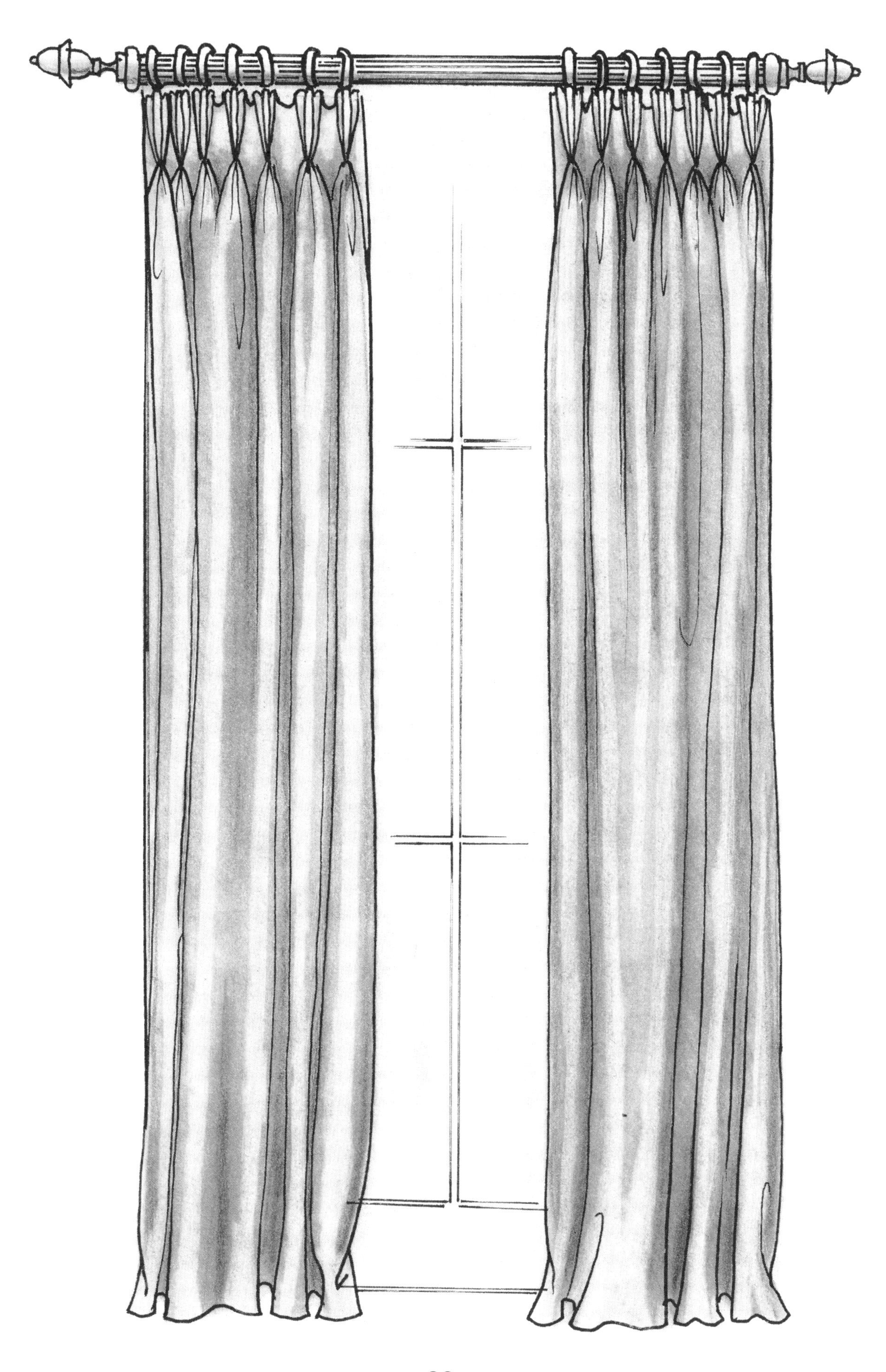

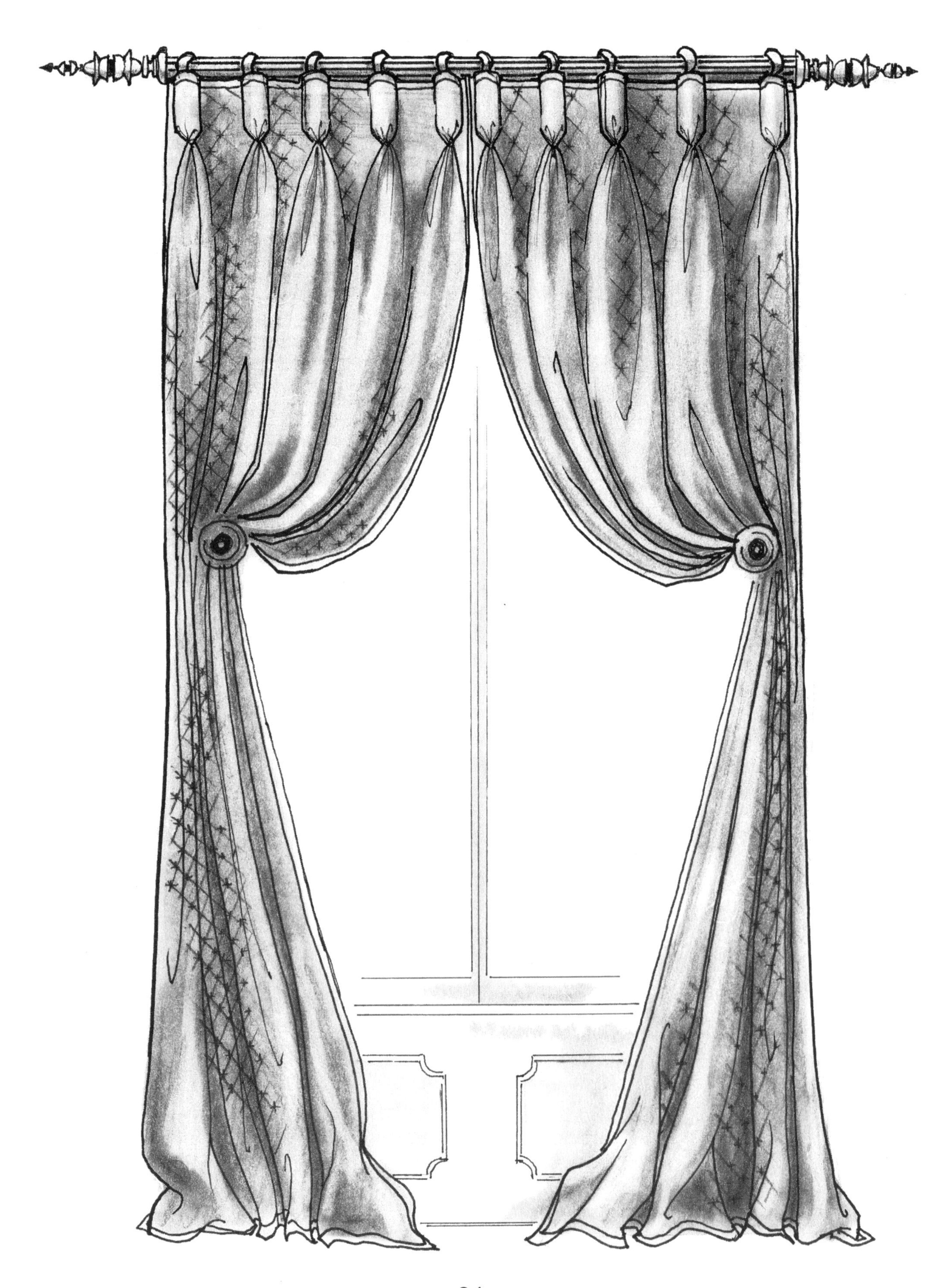

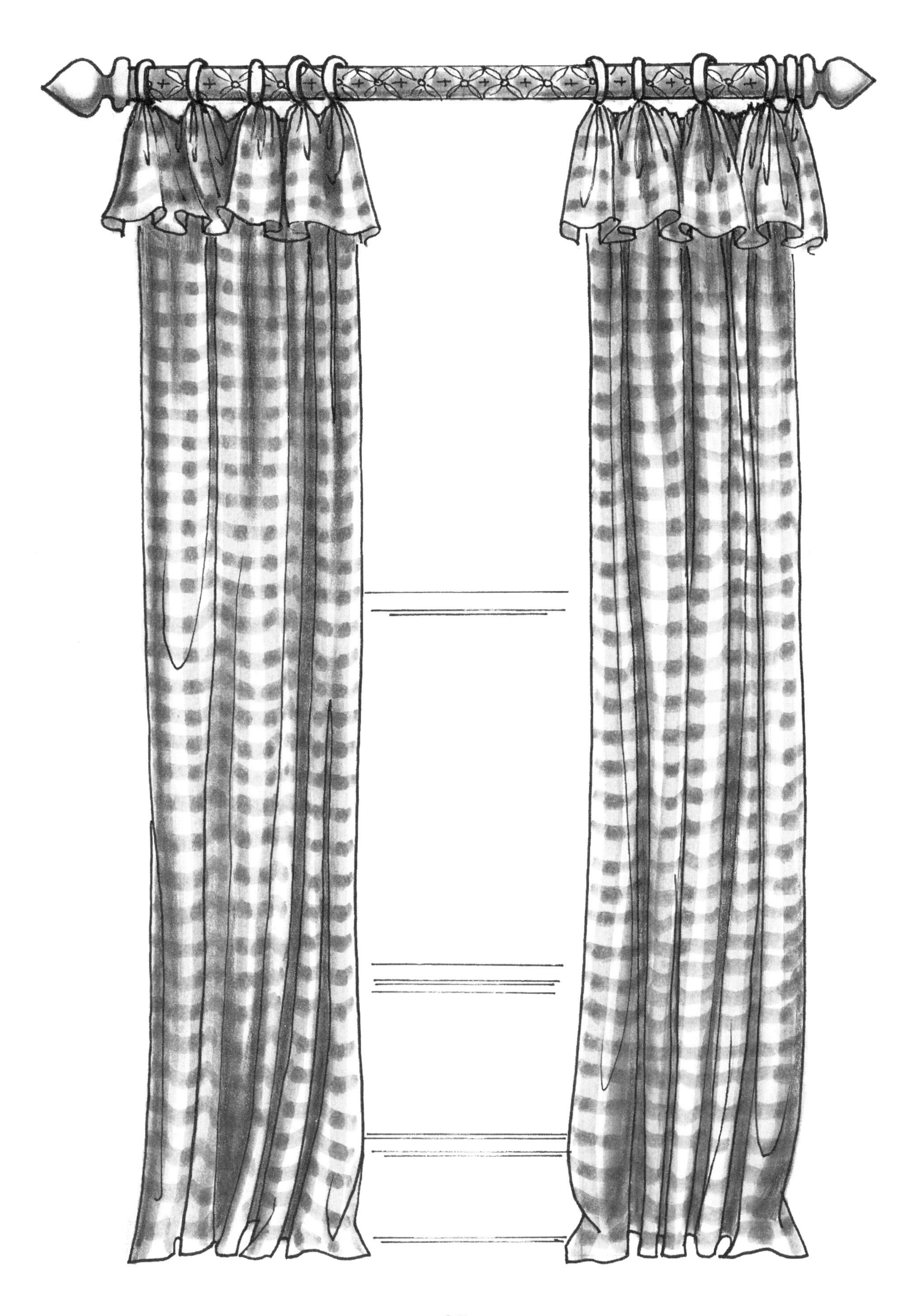

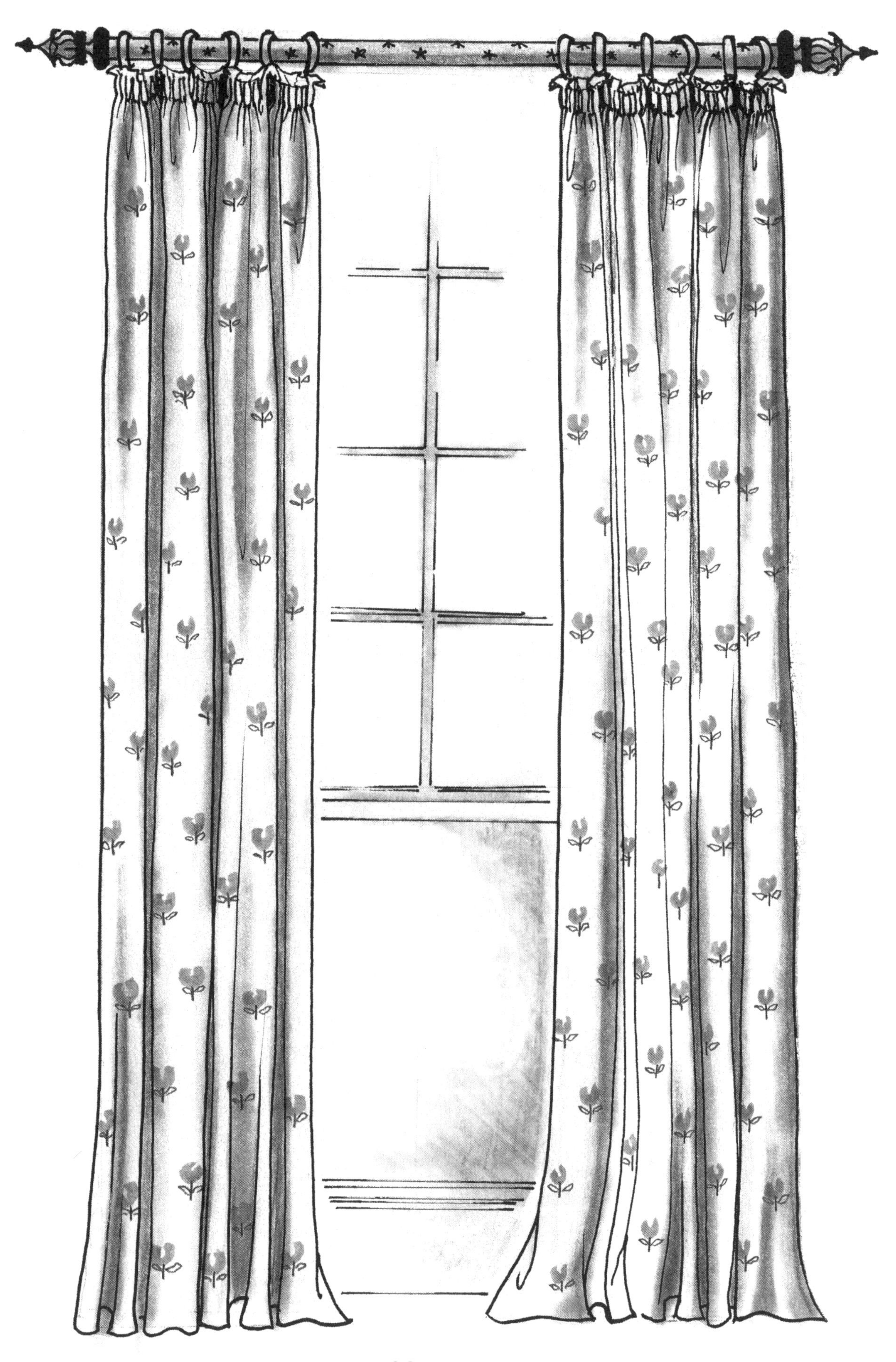

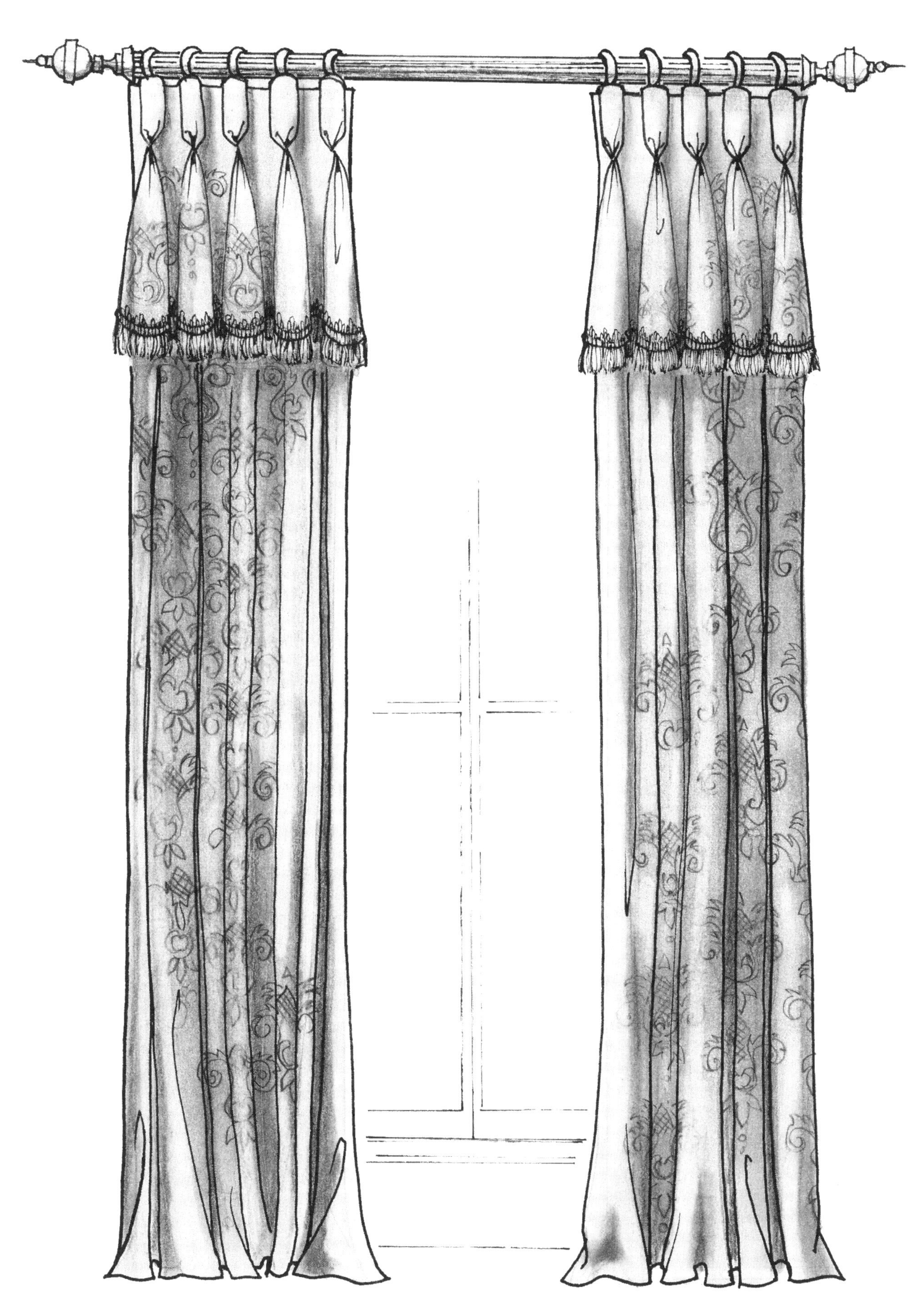

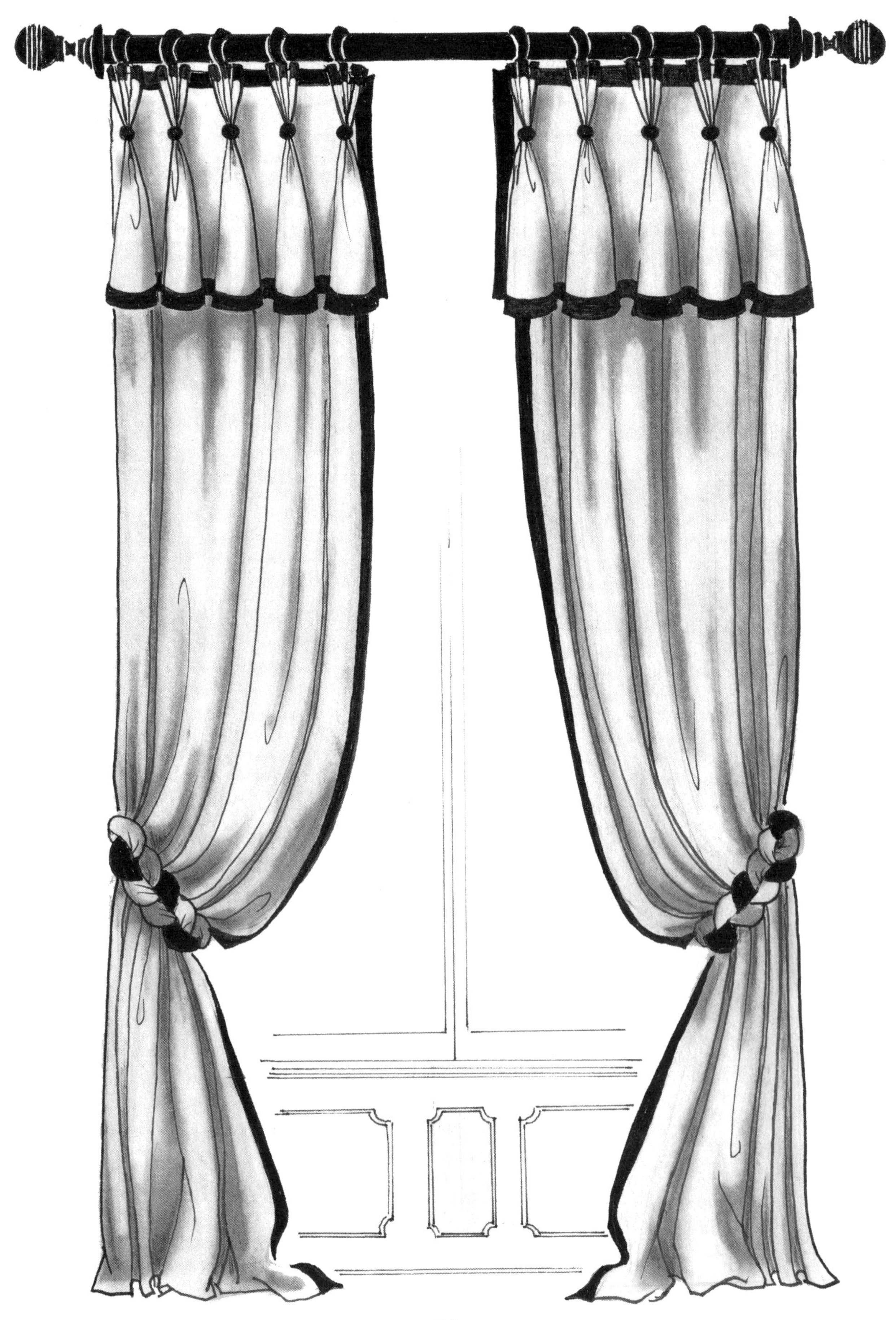

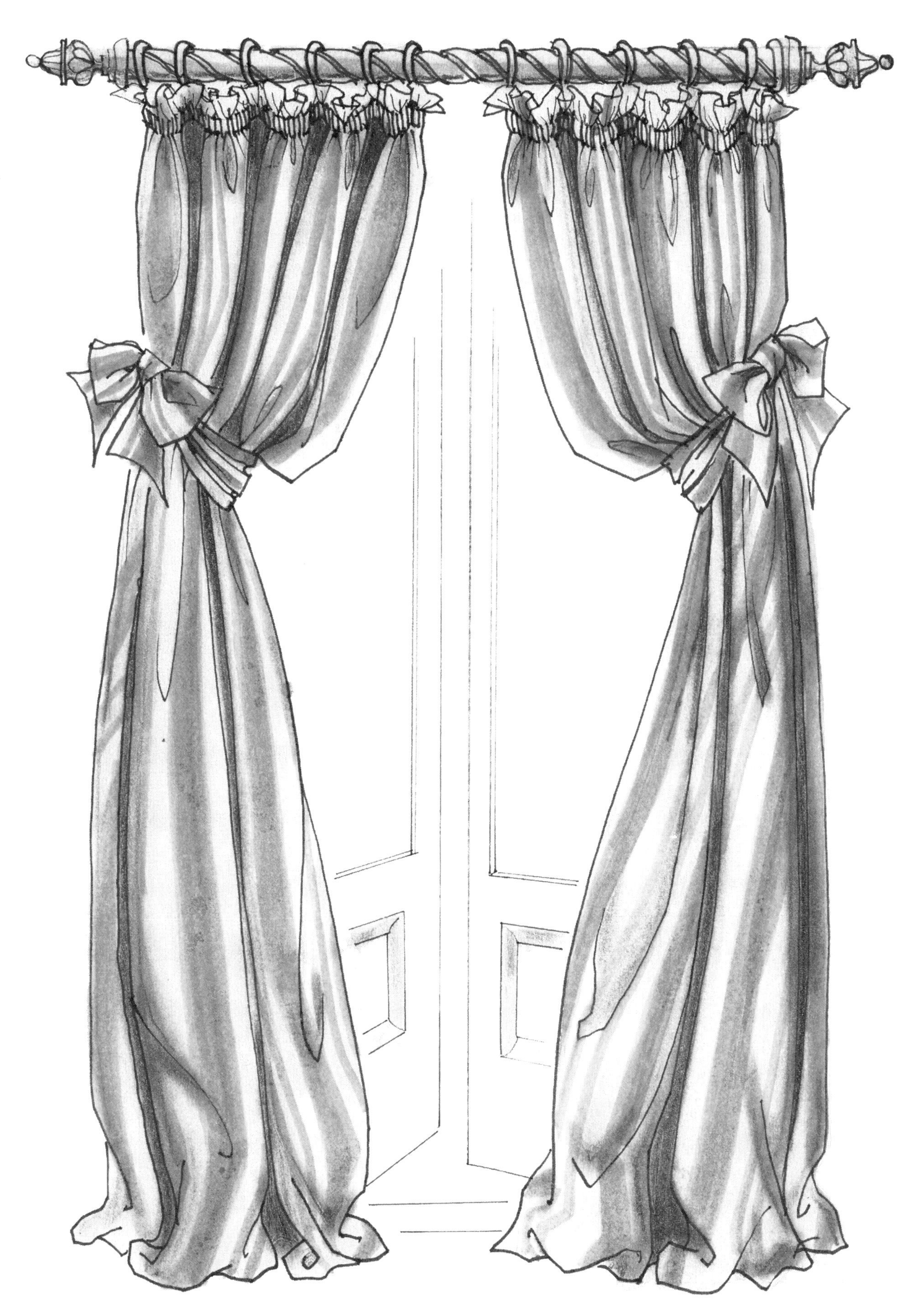

Curtains with valances

The designs on the next few pages need that little extra – here I suggest interlining with PRESHRUNK TWILL and finish by lining with CHROMAX crease resist lining.

Use DOMETTE as usual, in the valances as it is easy to manage in the workroom and does give a very professional finish.

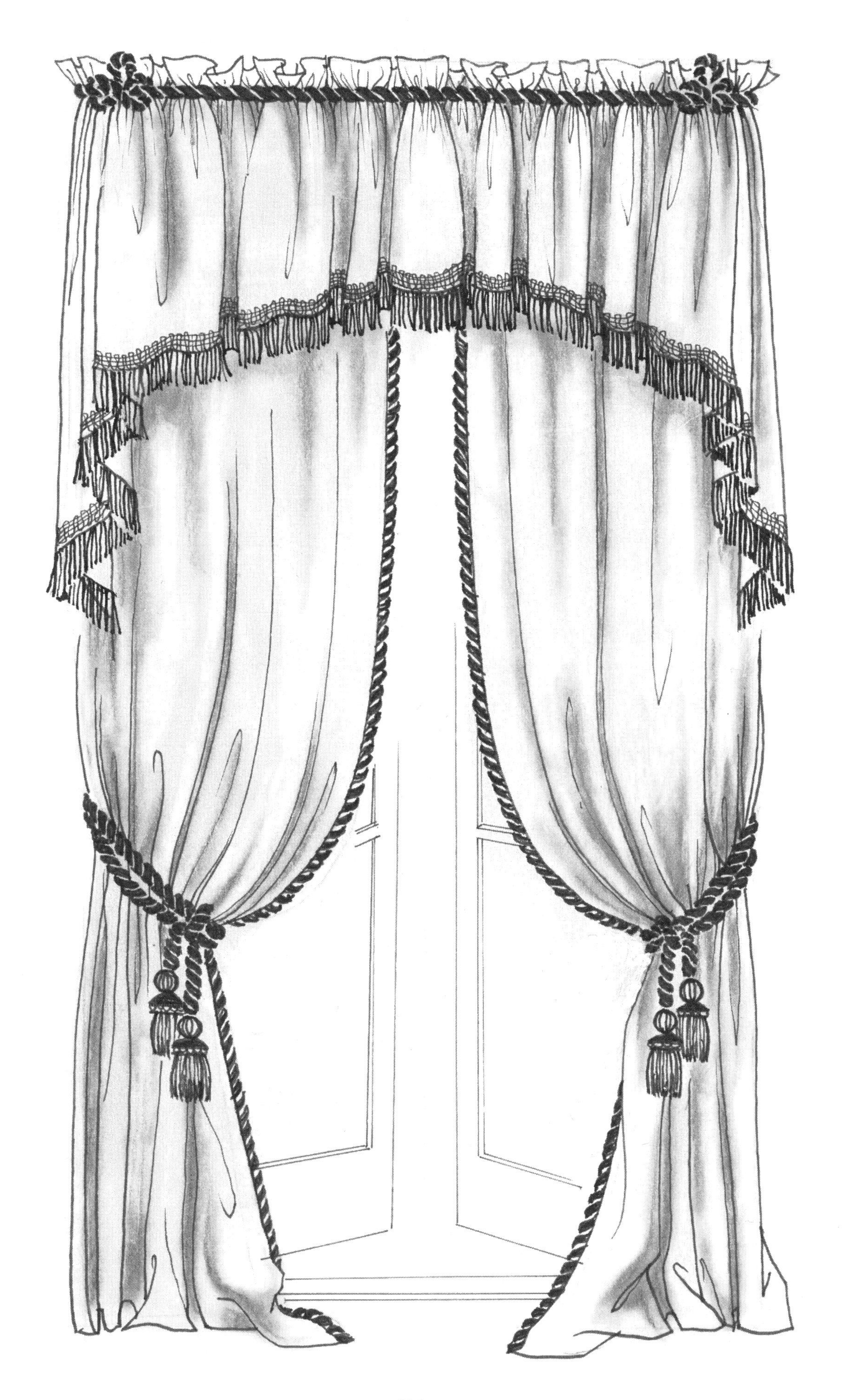

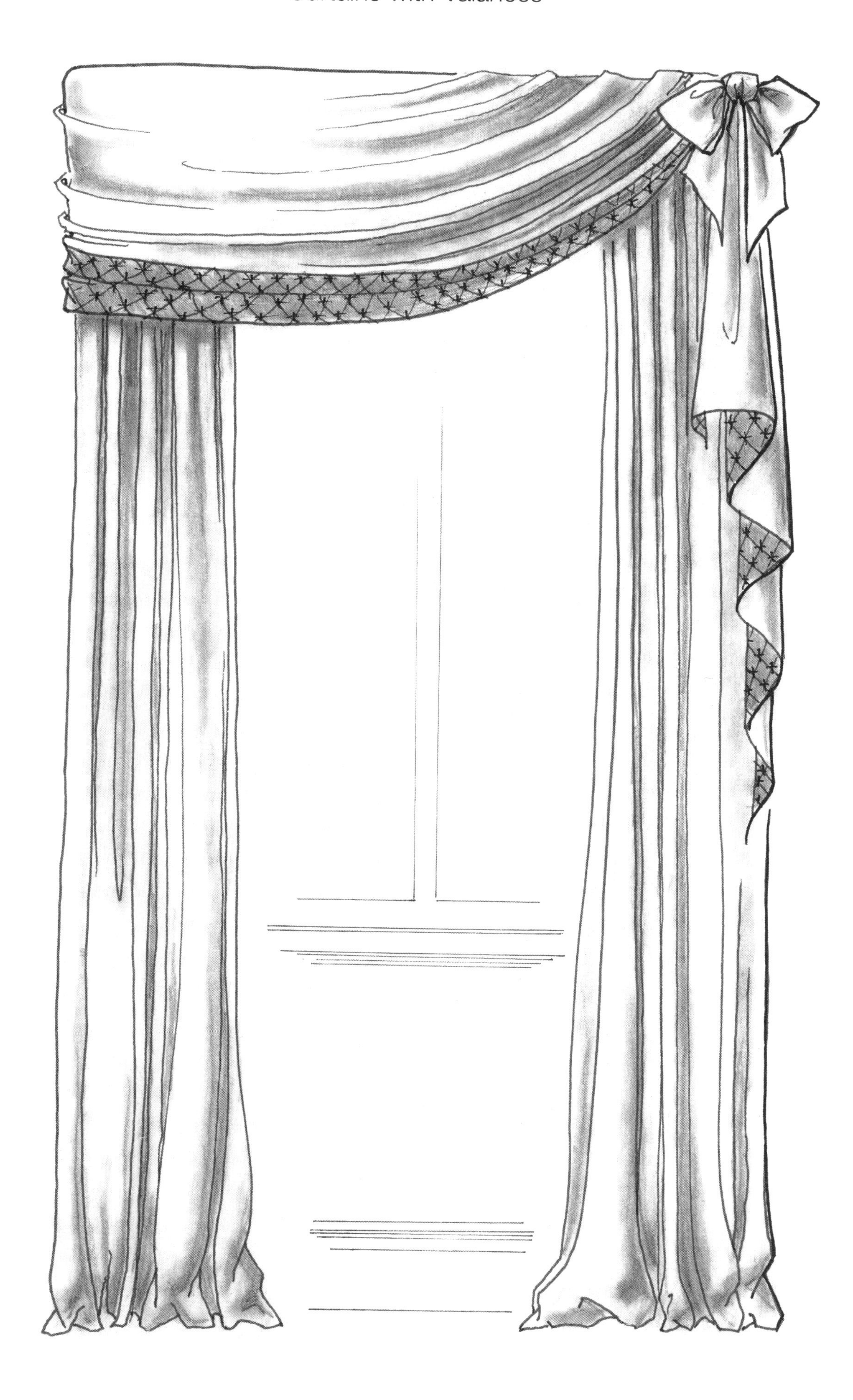

Curtains with Pelmets

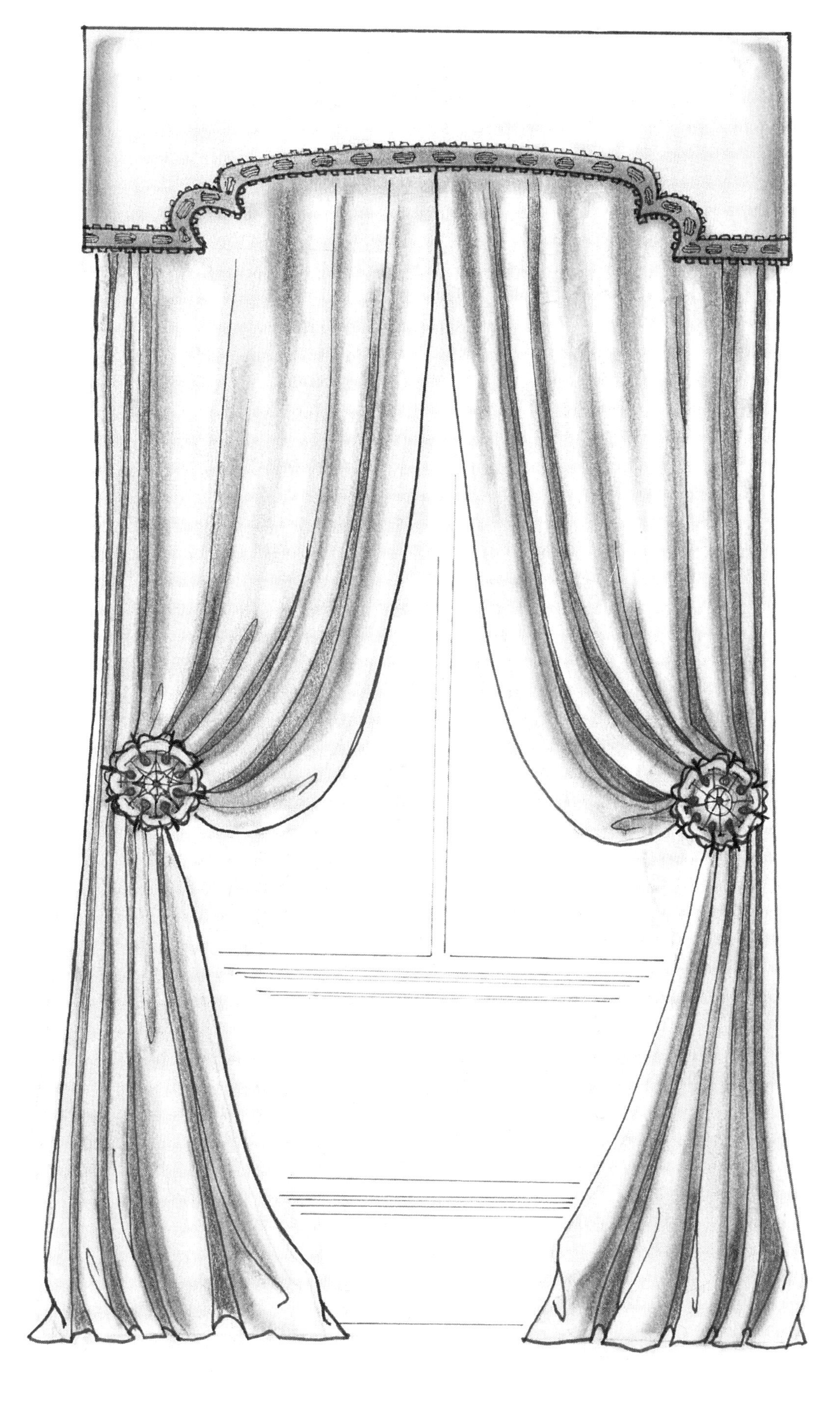

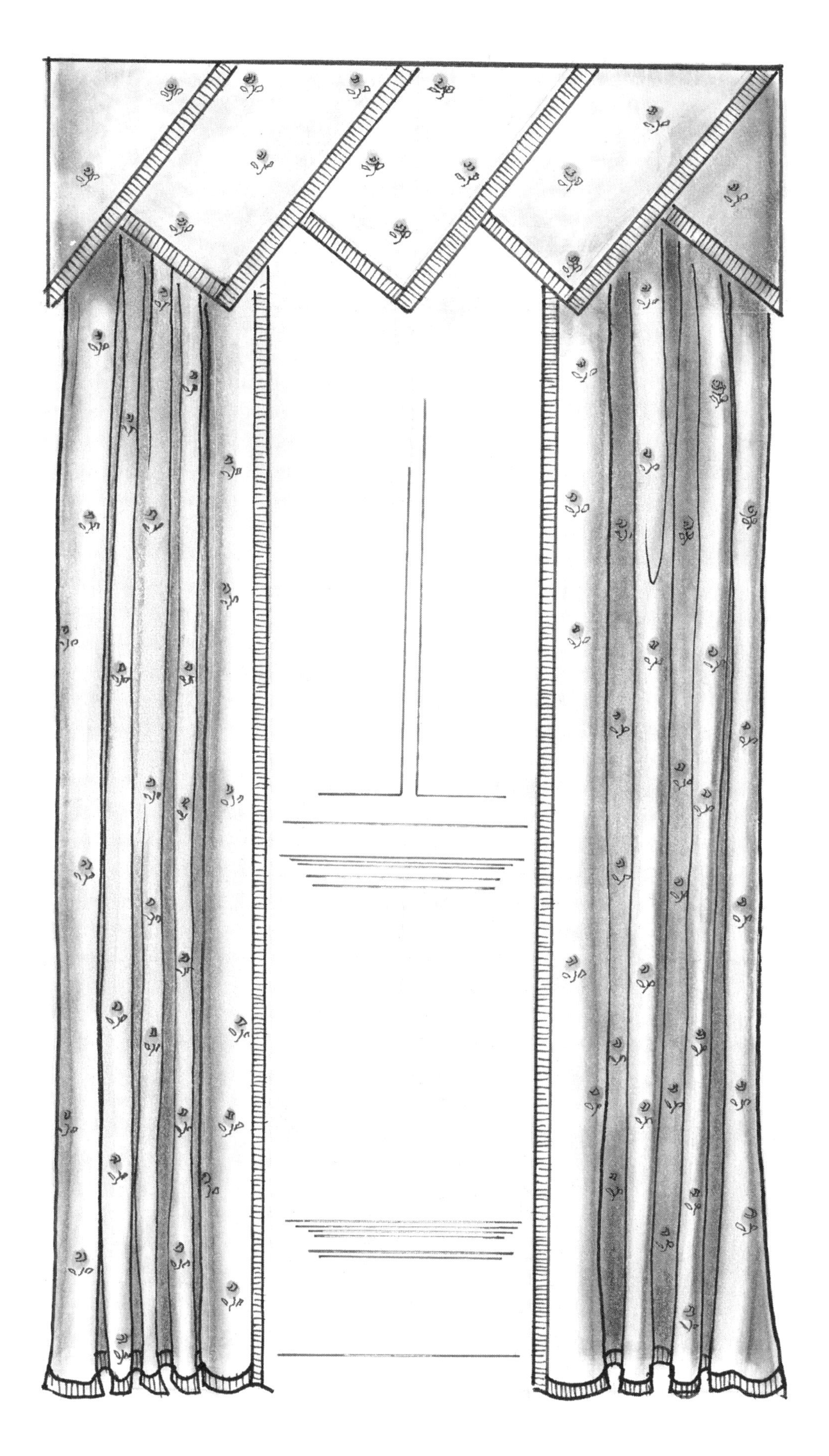

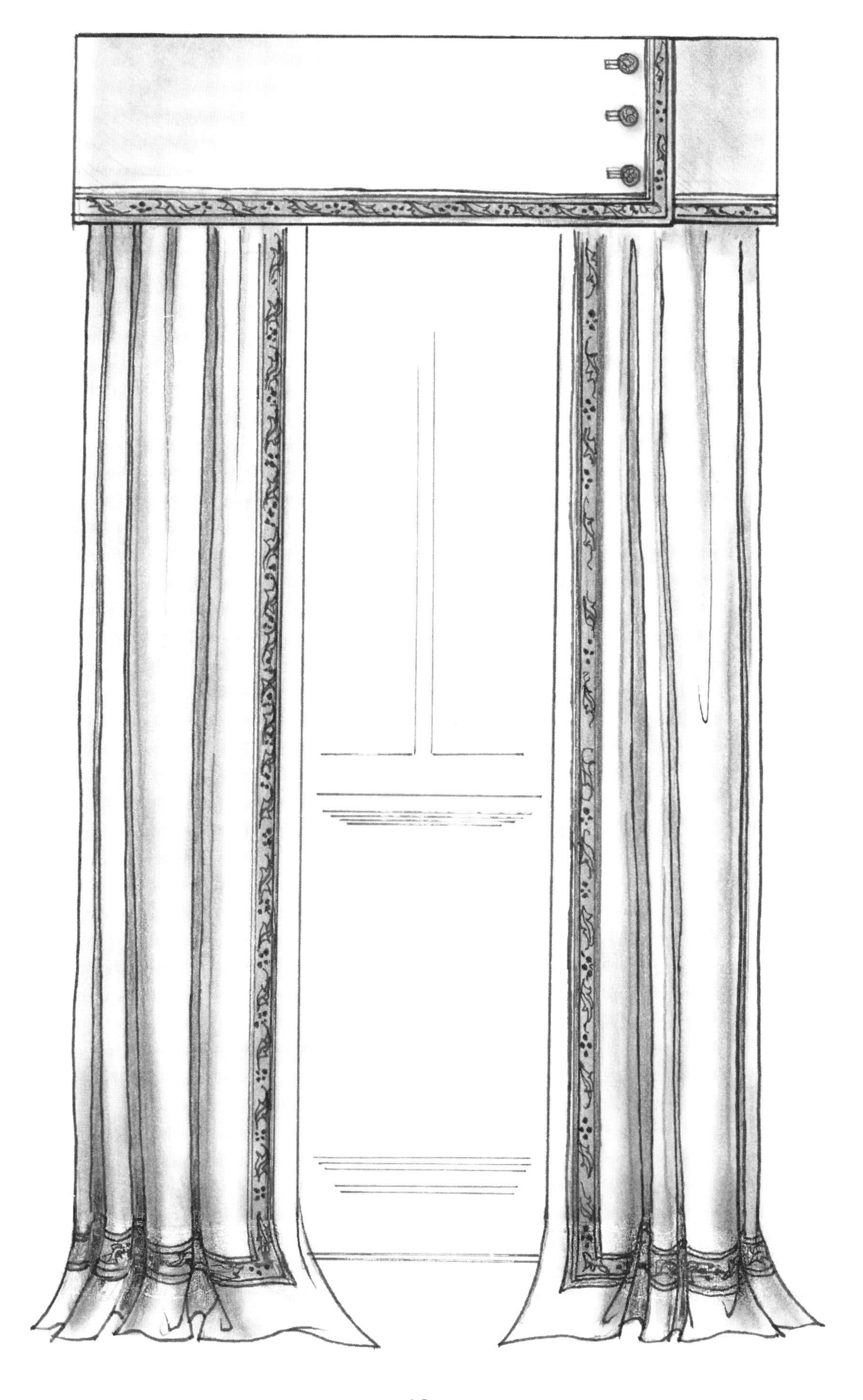

Formal curtains and swags and tails

The next few pages are filled with really opulent designs – use plenty of luscious fabrics and trim with beads or cut fringing.

Only the best is right here so I suggest using NATURAL BUMP to give it that extra thickness and then line with PLATINUM crease resist lining.

Once again, for the interlining of the soft drapes in the swags and tails – use DOMETTE.

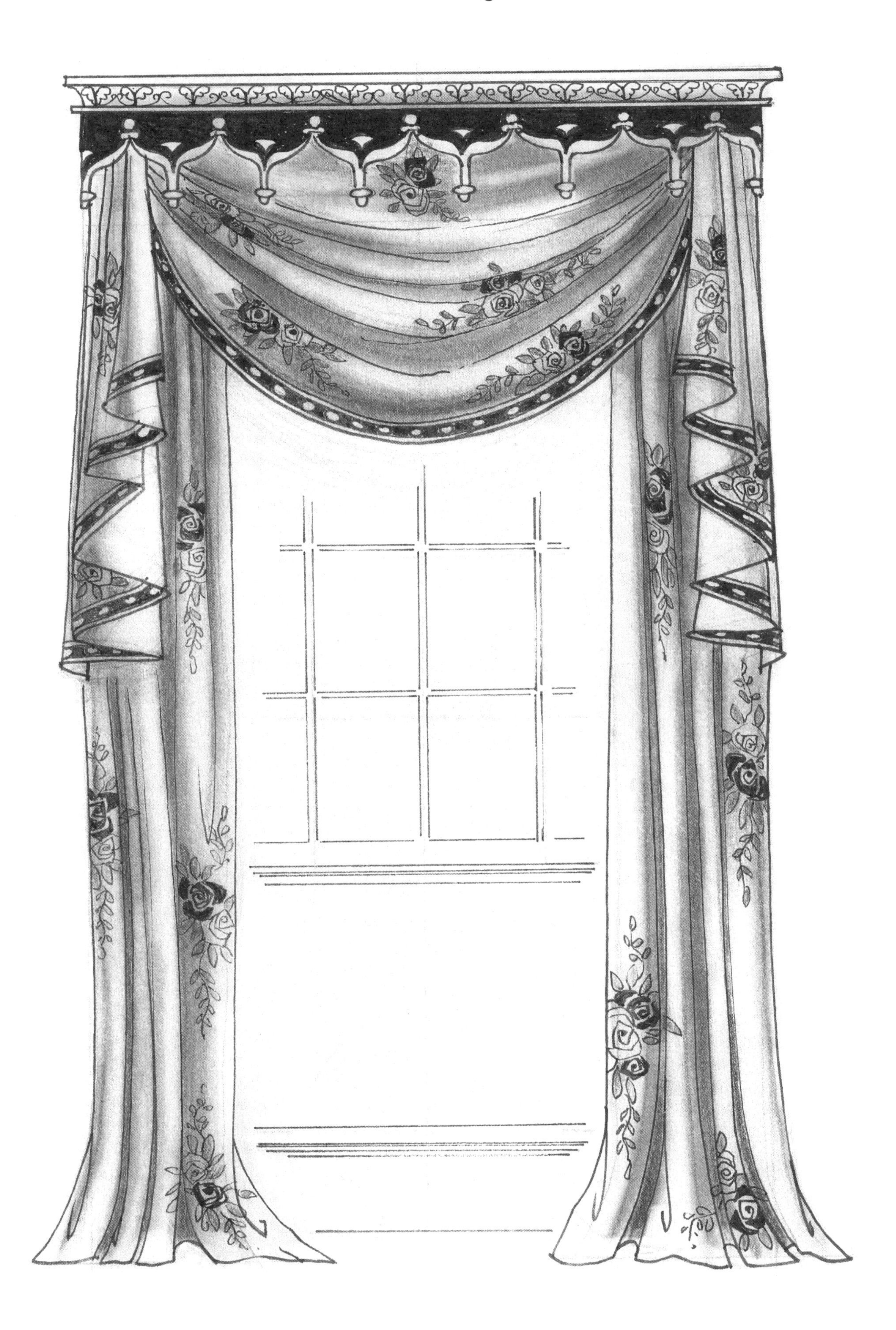

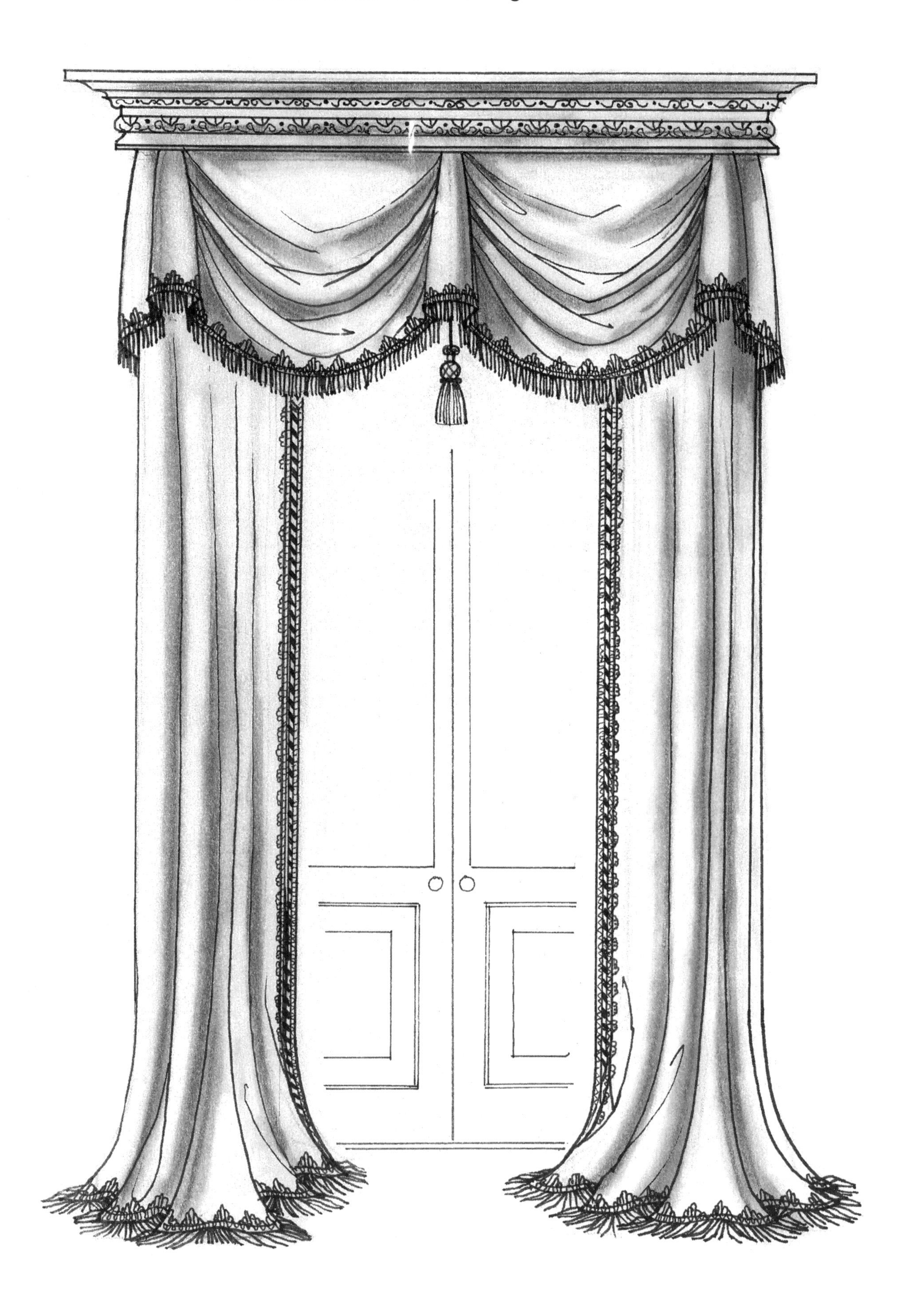

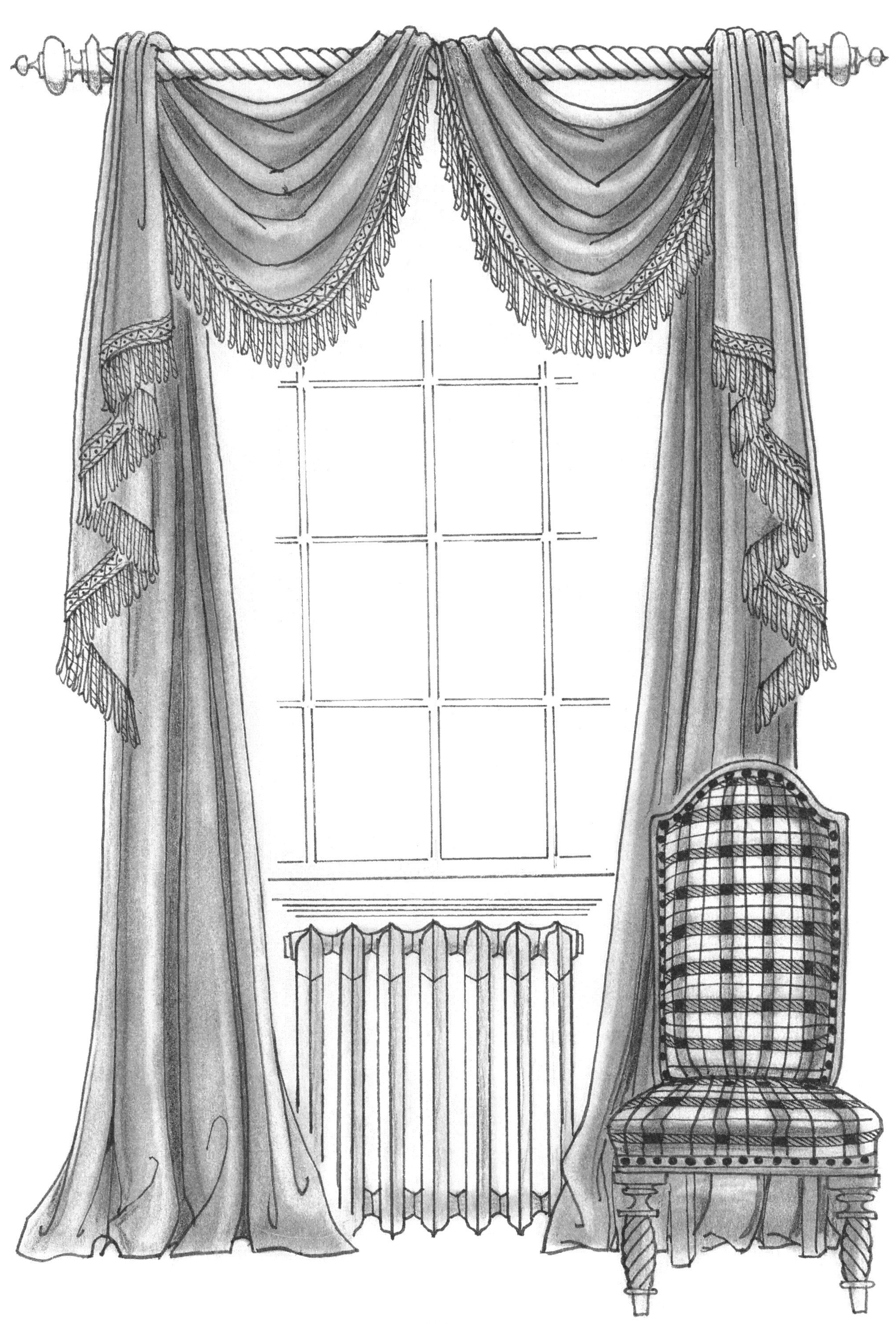

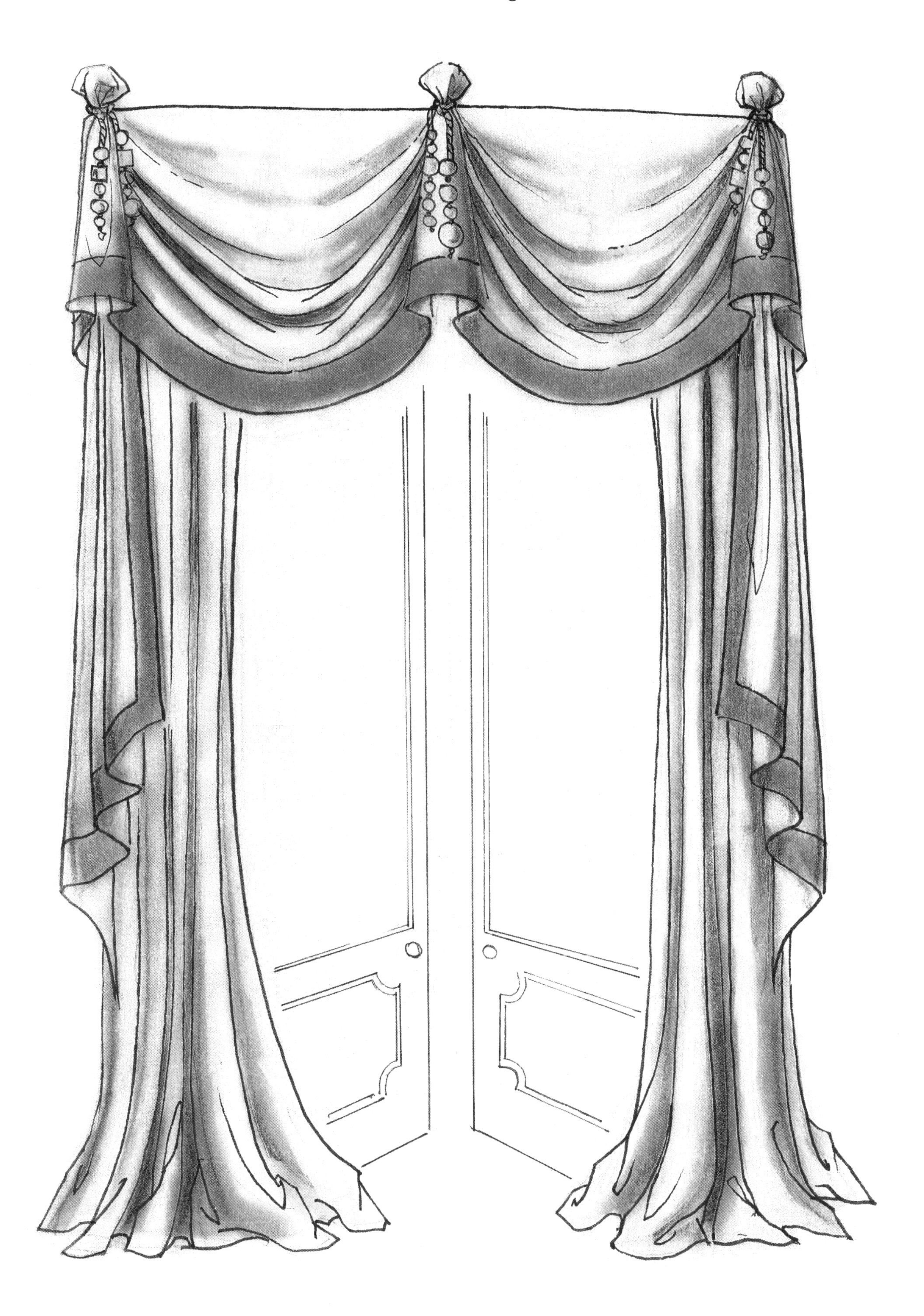

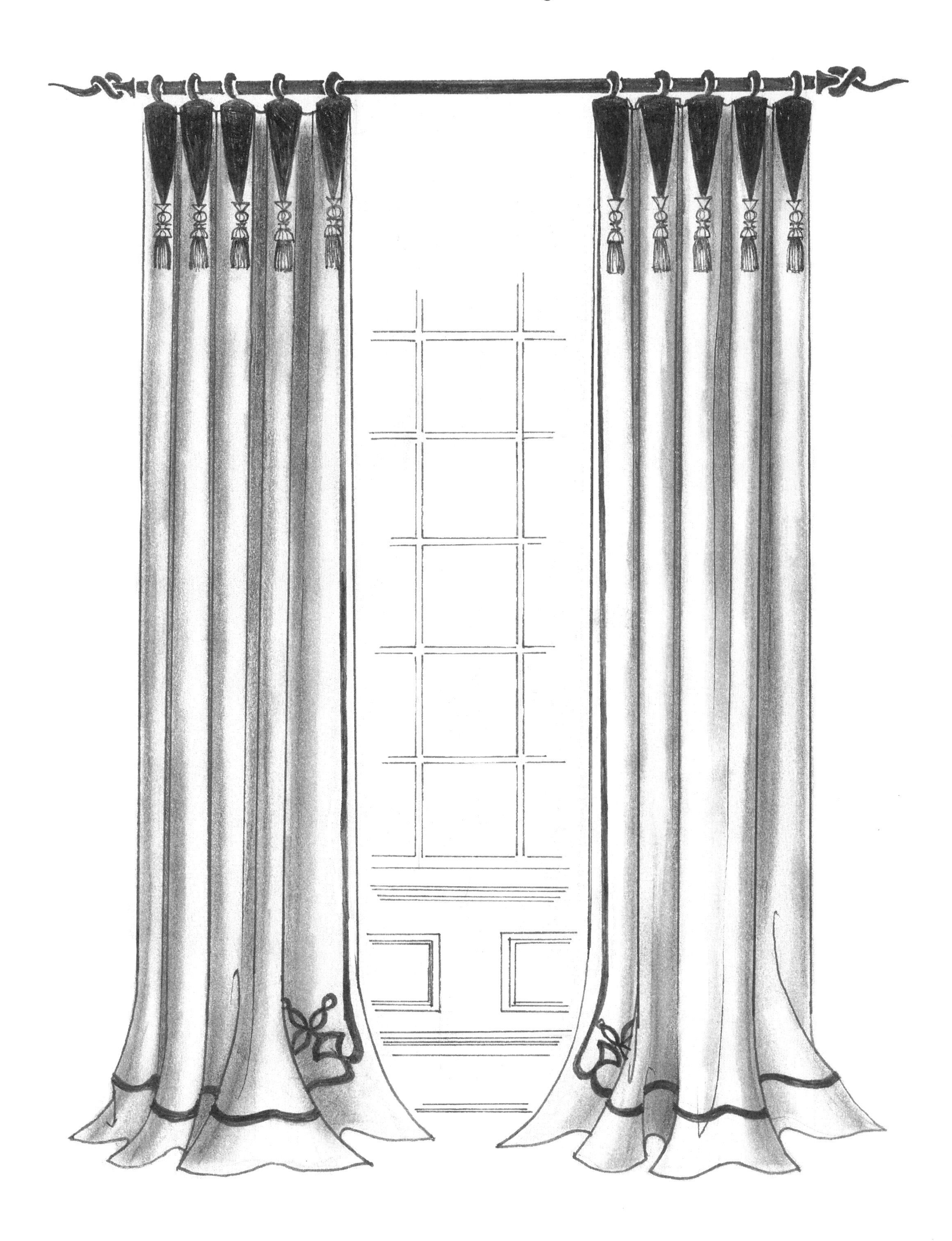

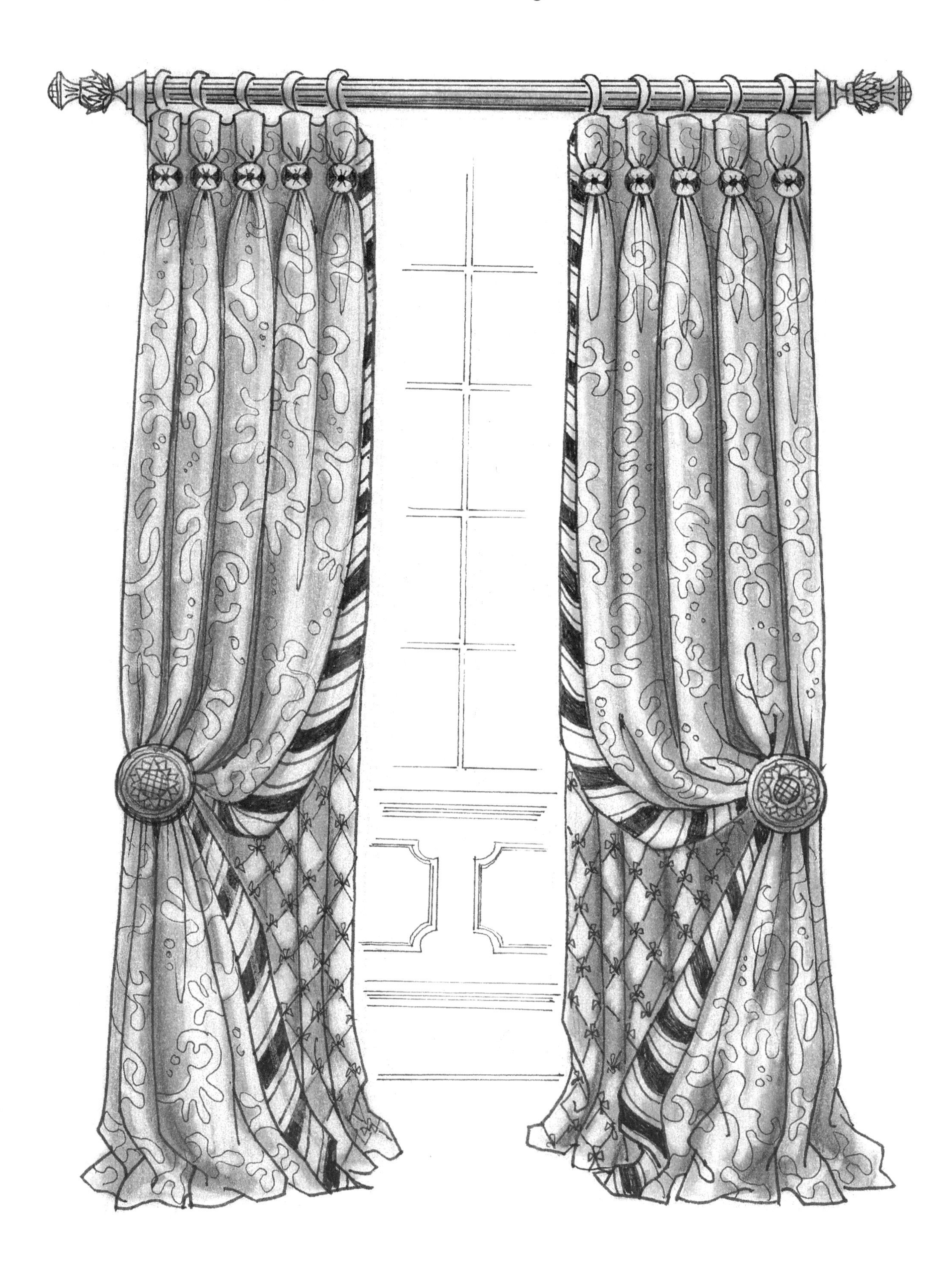

Minimal look

Keep the lines of the curtains on the next pages really SIMPLE – you could use SONATA COTTON CHINZ for the contrast edging on some of the designs to emphasize the line of the design and then line with one of the CHROMAX neutral SATEEN linings.

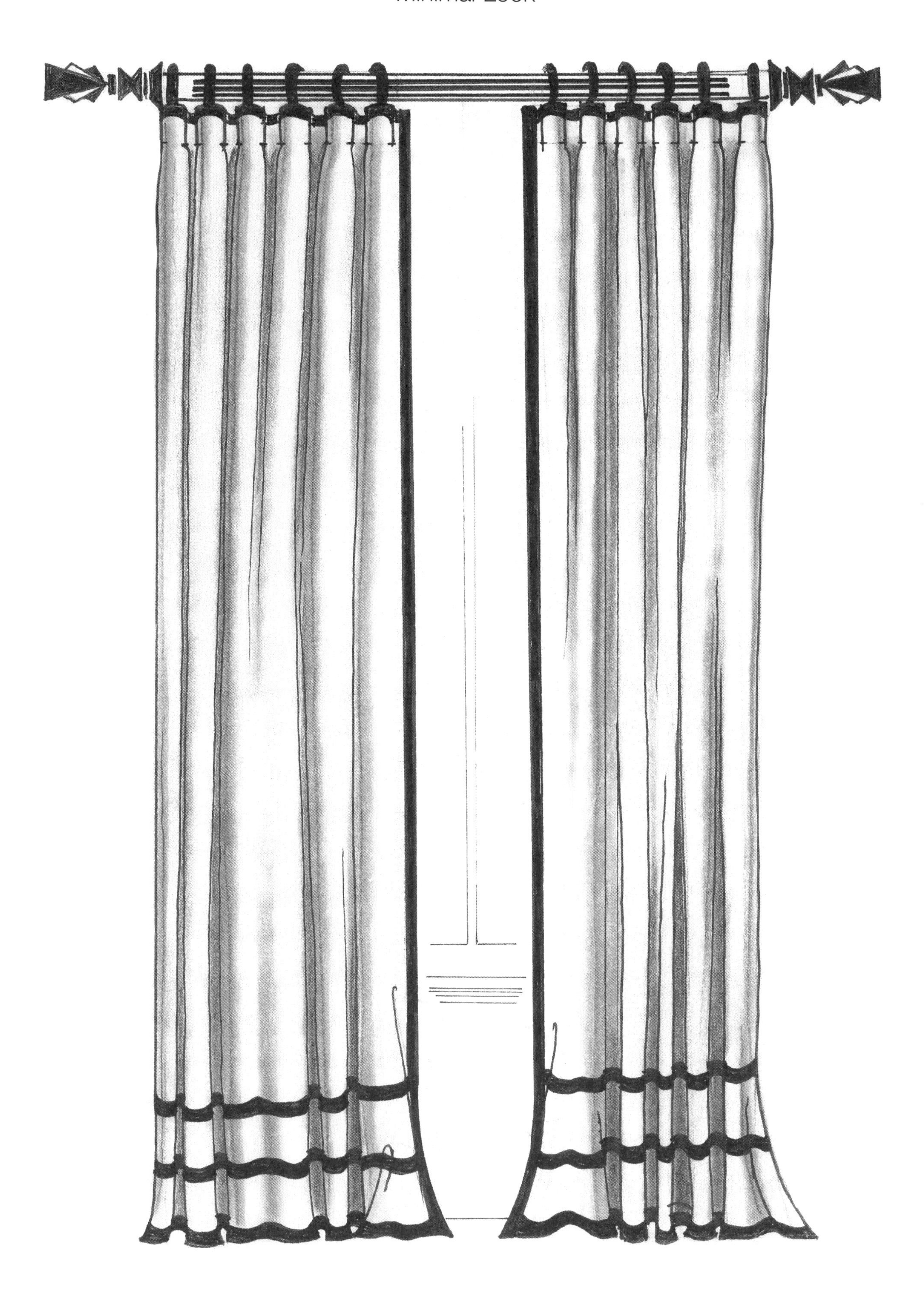

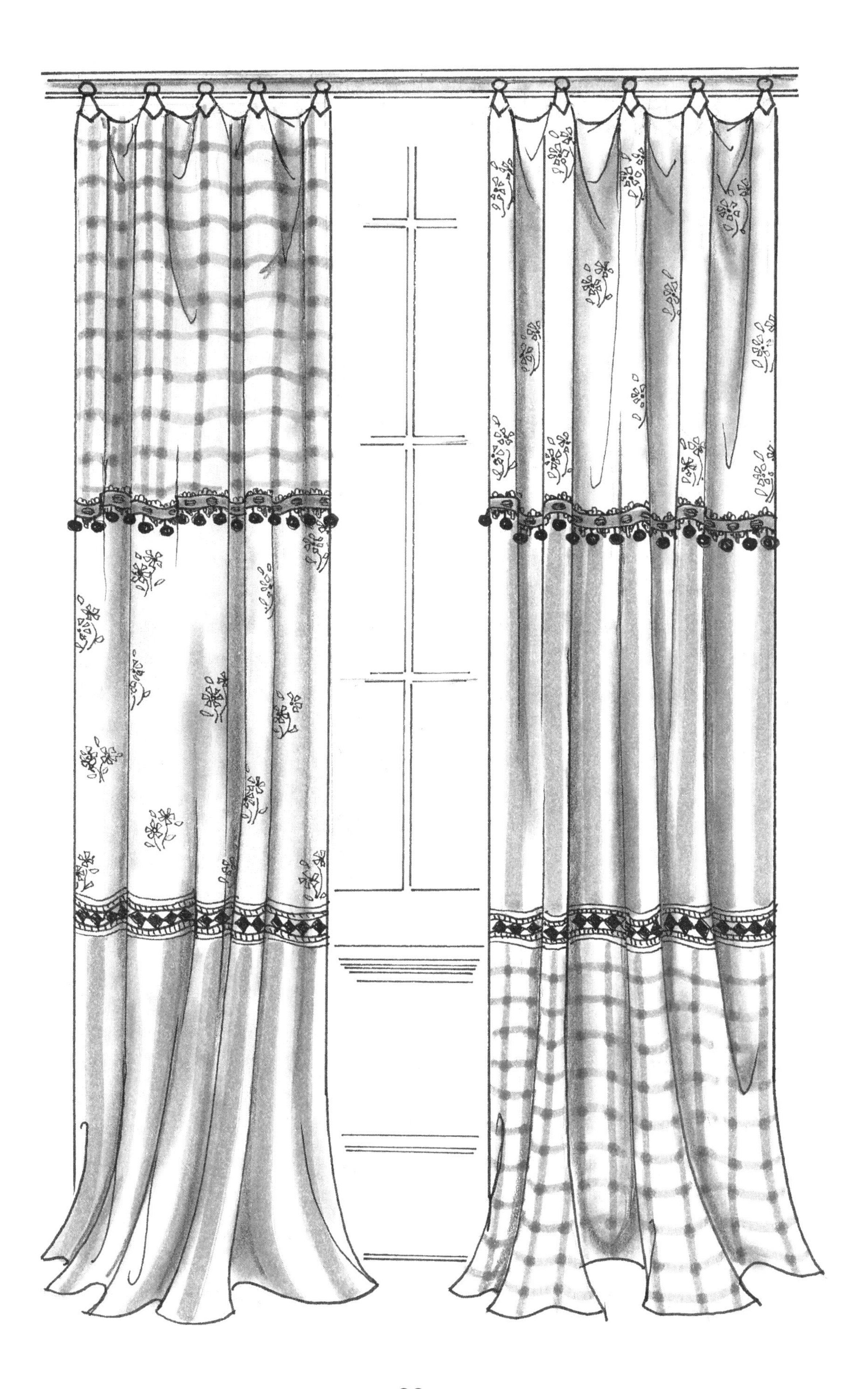

Minimal Look

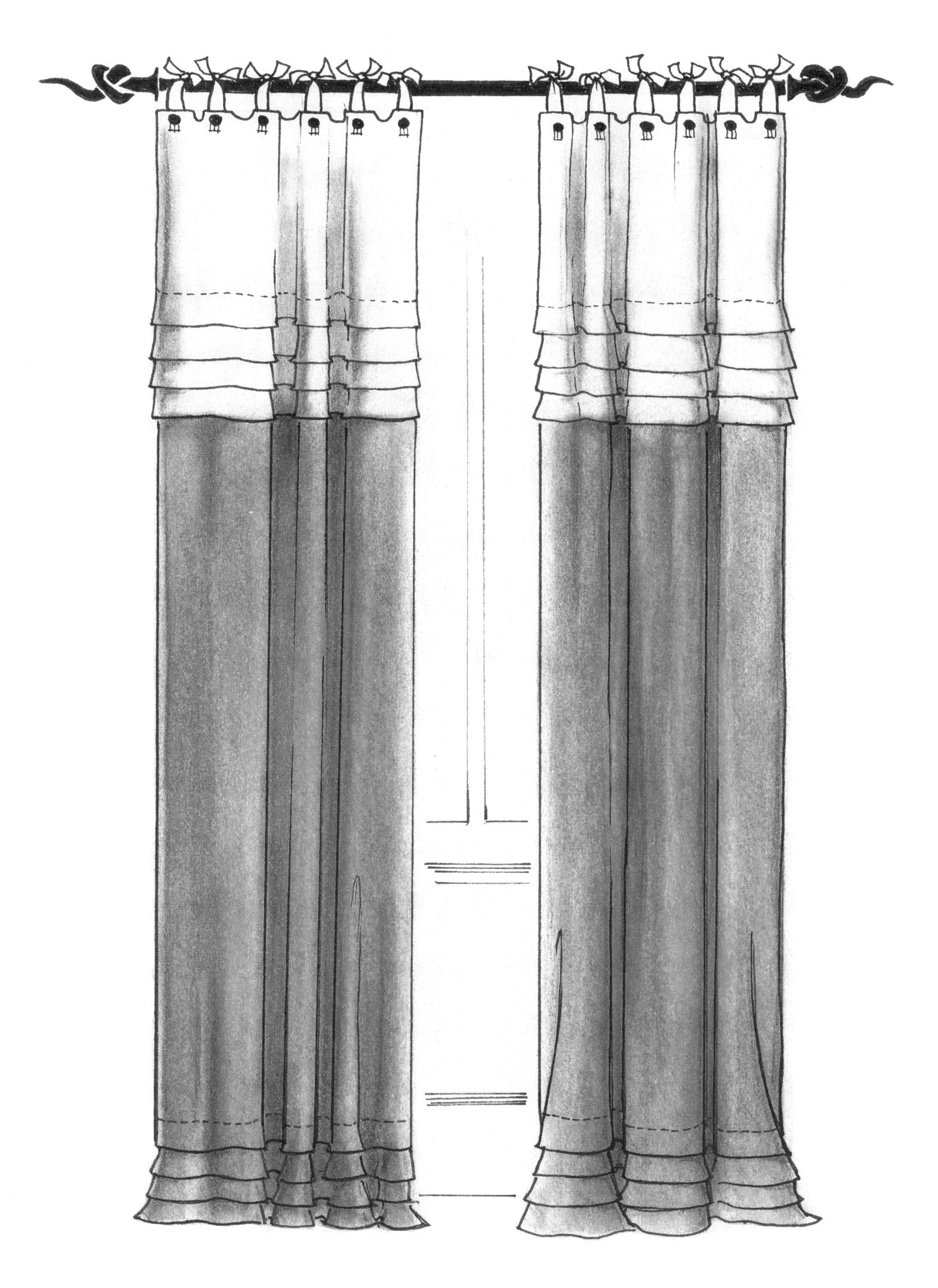

Bay Windows

One of the main problems with bay windows is that you often end up by losing too much light when you have a lot of fabric, so here it would be best to use SYNTHETIC interlining to allow the curtains to stack neatly without being too bulky.

Towards the end of this section there are some 'dress curtains' with blinds make your own choice of INTERMAX interlining from a wide selection of different weights for the curtains and use the SYNTHETIC lining again for the blinds.

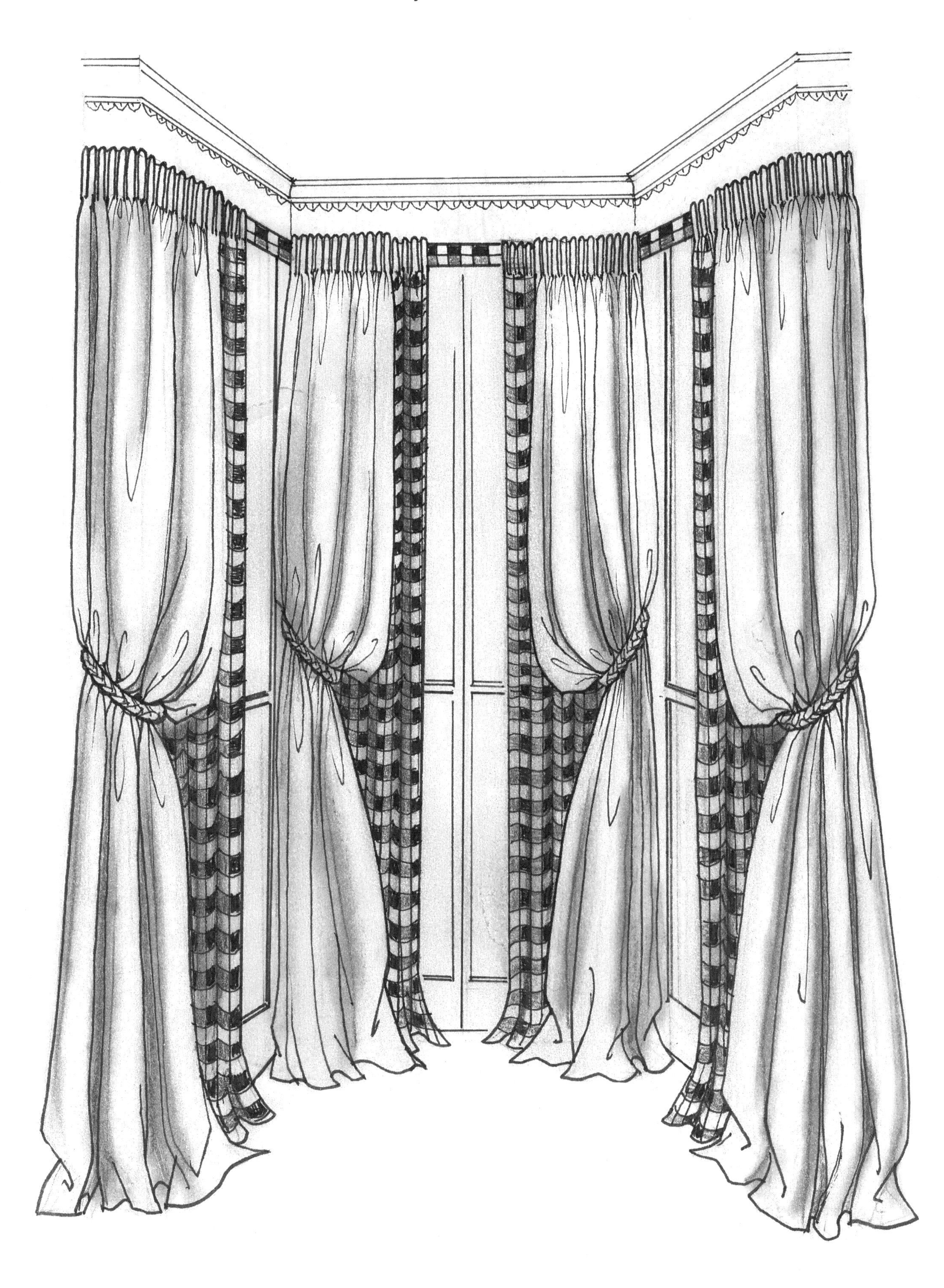

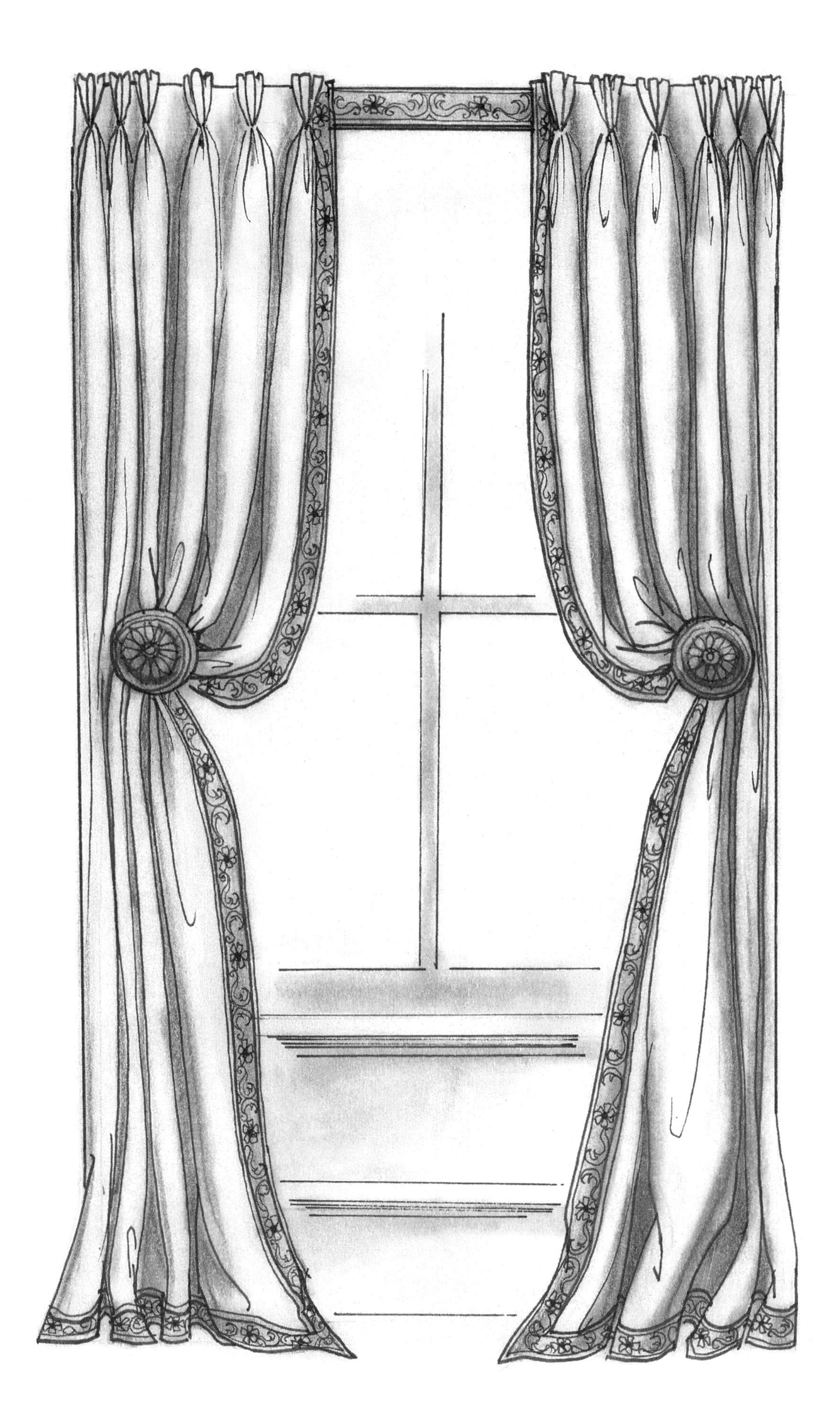

Italian Strung

These Italian strung curtains on the next few pages can sometimes look a disaster – so this is a good time to use the CASCADE coloured linings to finish off your curtains – then it doesn't matter if the lining is showing – there is an excellent colour range to choose from – match the lining to your fabric which will help to add a wonderful theatrical effect of these dramatic curtains.

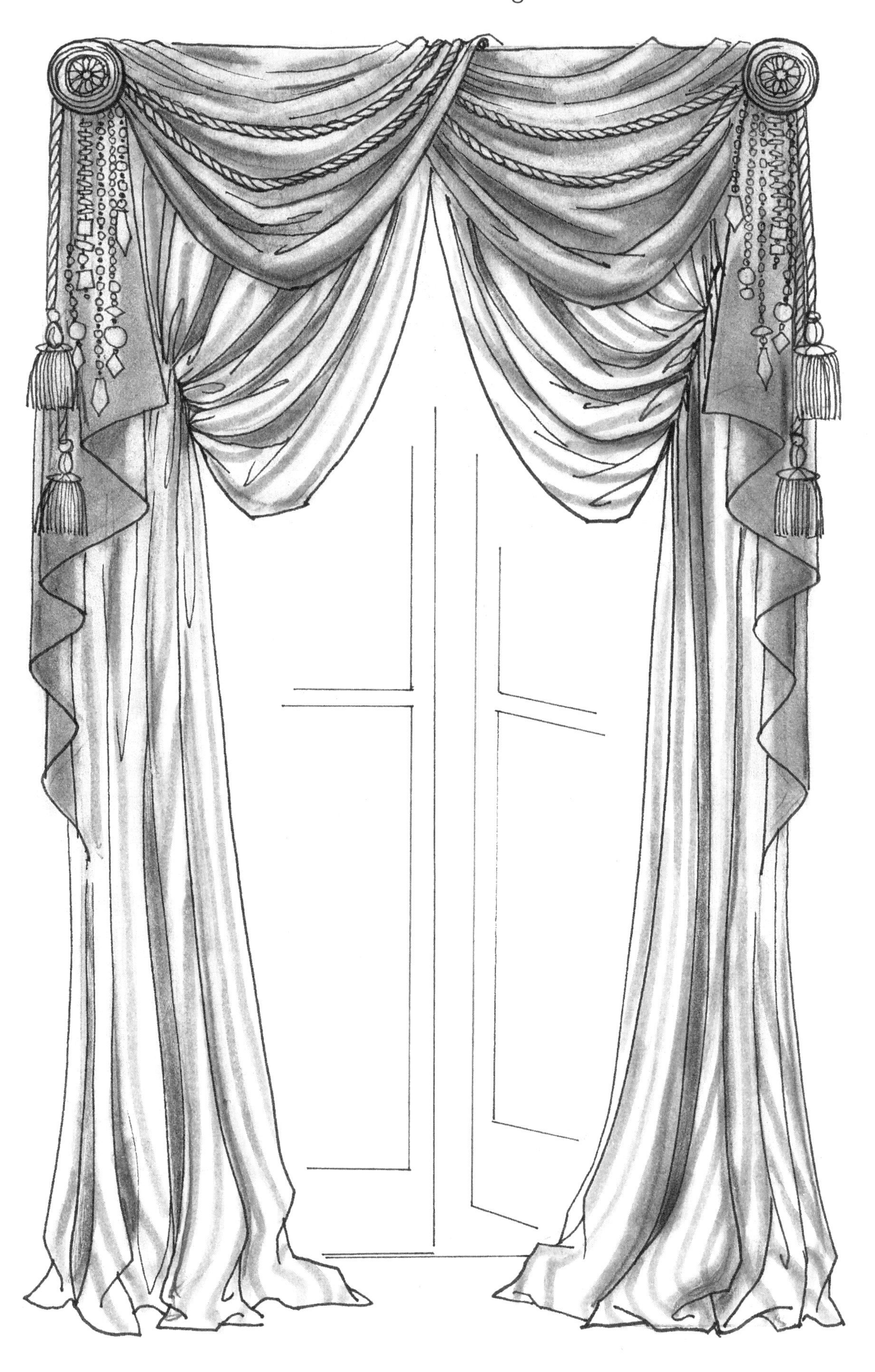

Italian Strung

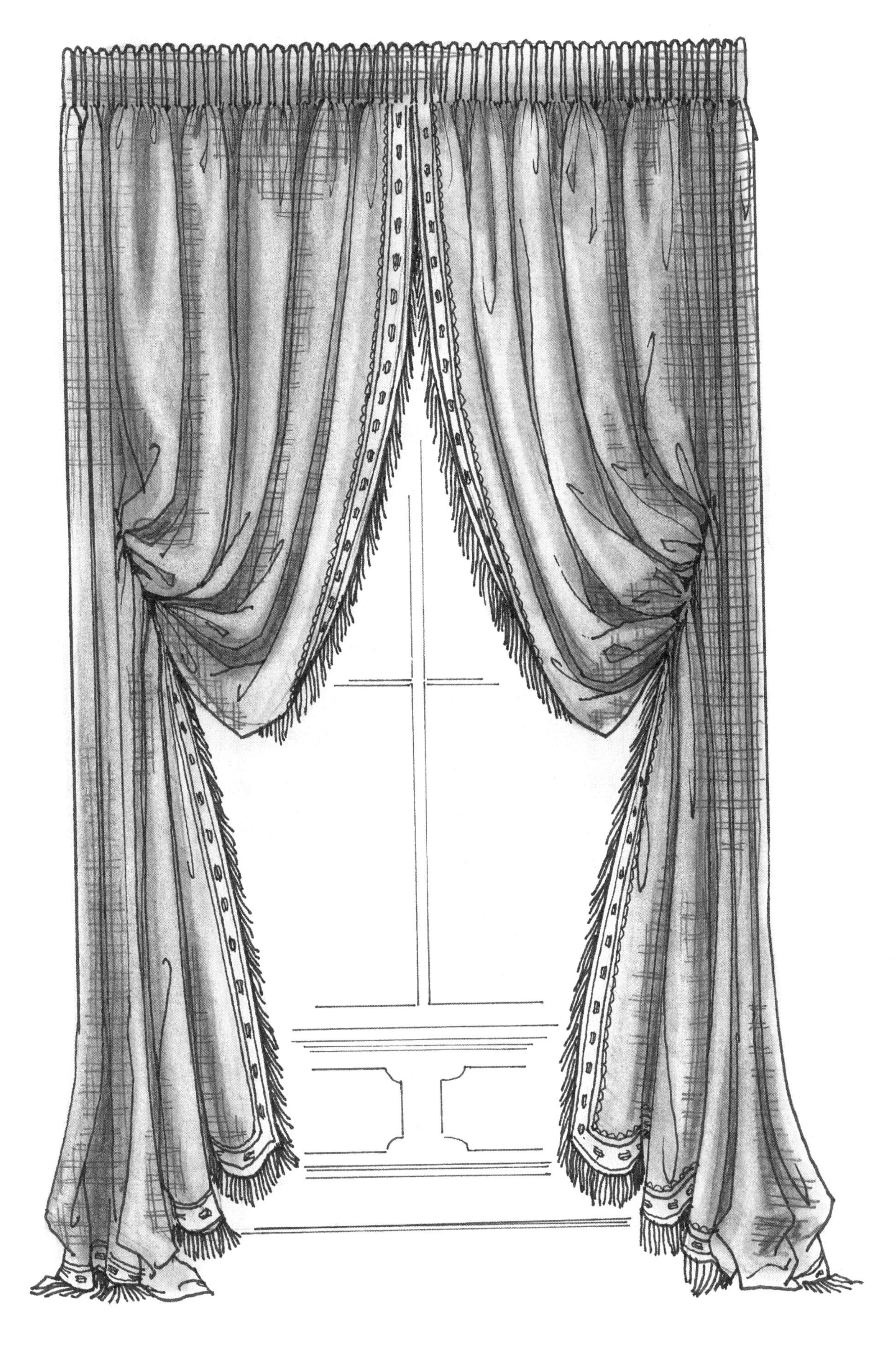

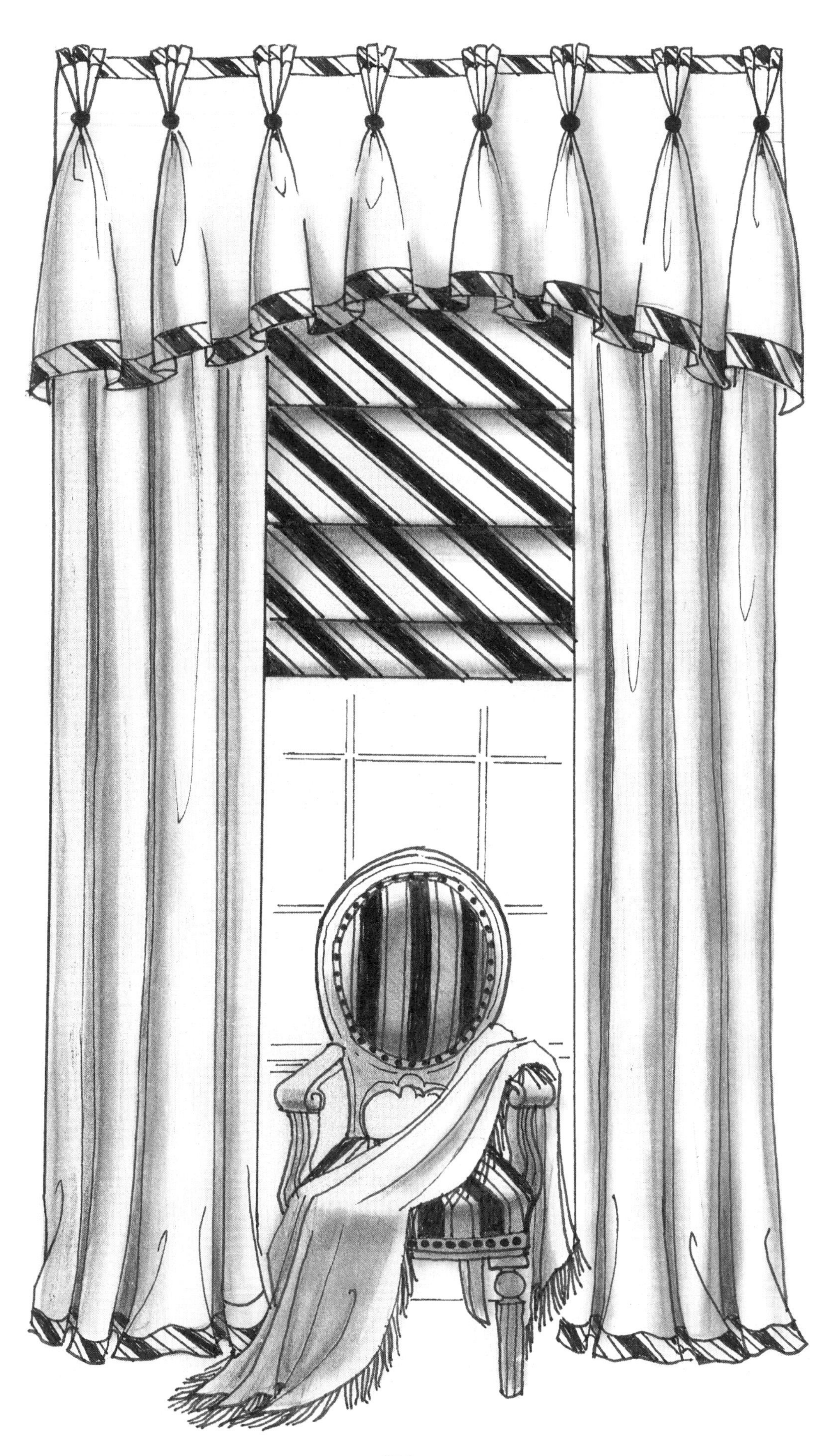

Bedroom curtains

Most people given the choice, prefer BLACKOUT lining in their bedrooms – so here I suggest using OLYMPIA BLACKOUT lining – it drapes beautifully and is easy to handle.

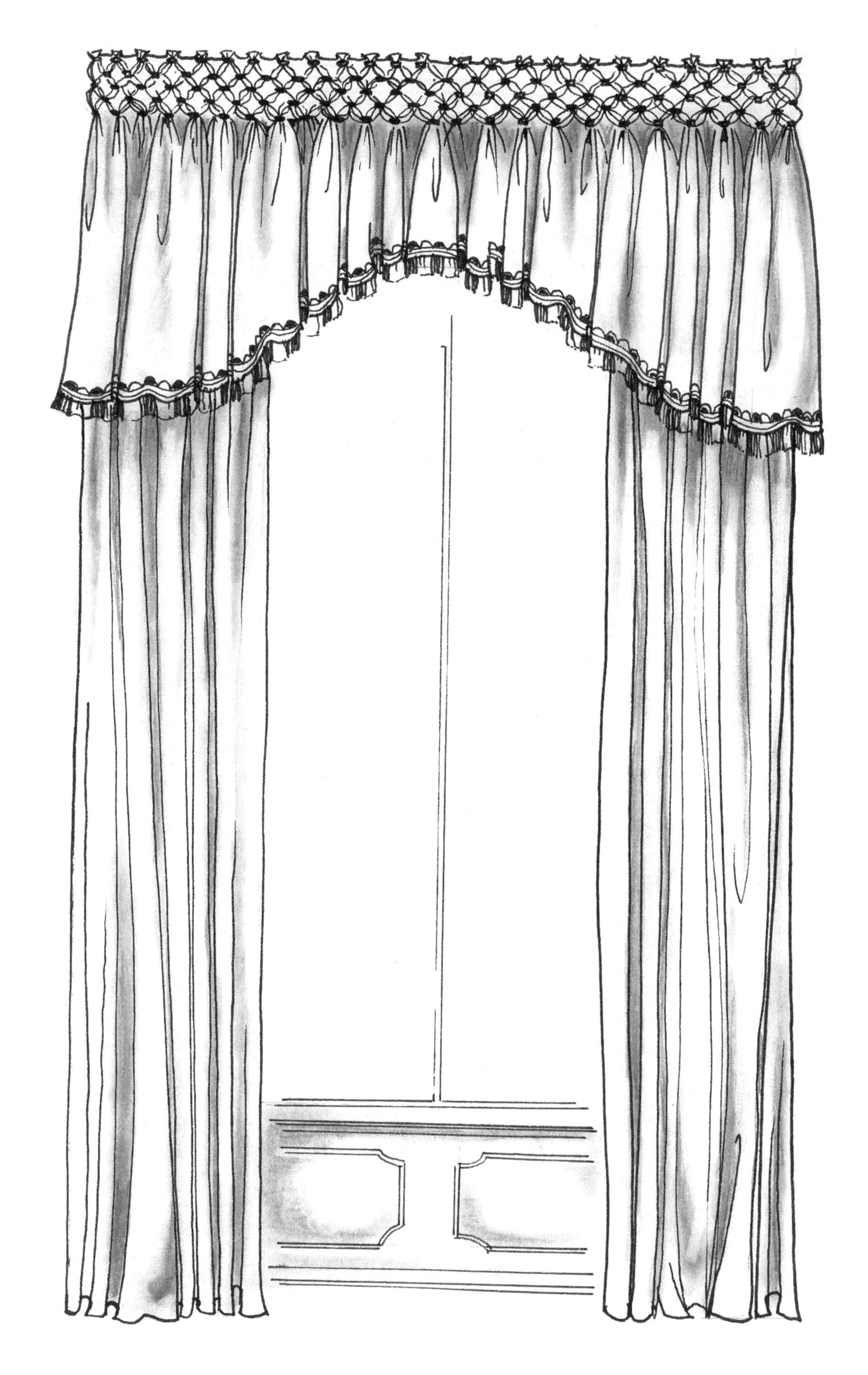

Portières

Just in case you live in a draughty castle – may I suggest using DUO LINING to keep out the draughts as well as adding a sumptuous look to the curtain – or if you feel you need to have a blackout lining for some reason try using OUTBLACK FLEECE because it also has the added THERMAL content too.

Blinds

When interlining Roman blinds you have a choice, either use OUTBLACK FLEECE as it lends stability to the blind or perhaps use a light weight SYNTHETIC INTERLINING and then finish off by using CHROMAX lining.

With Austrian blinds – simply use CHROMAX CASCADE to colour co-ordinate with your face fabric.

1

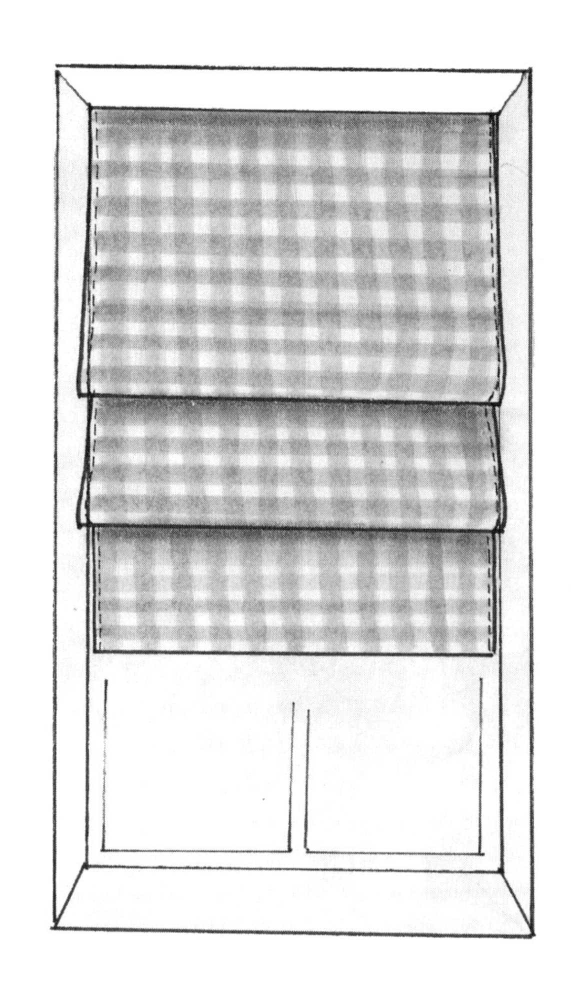

2

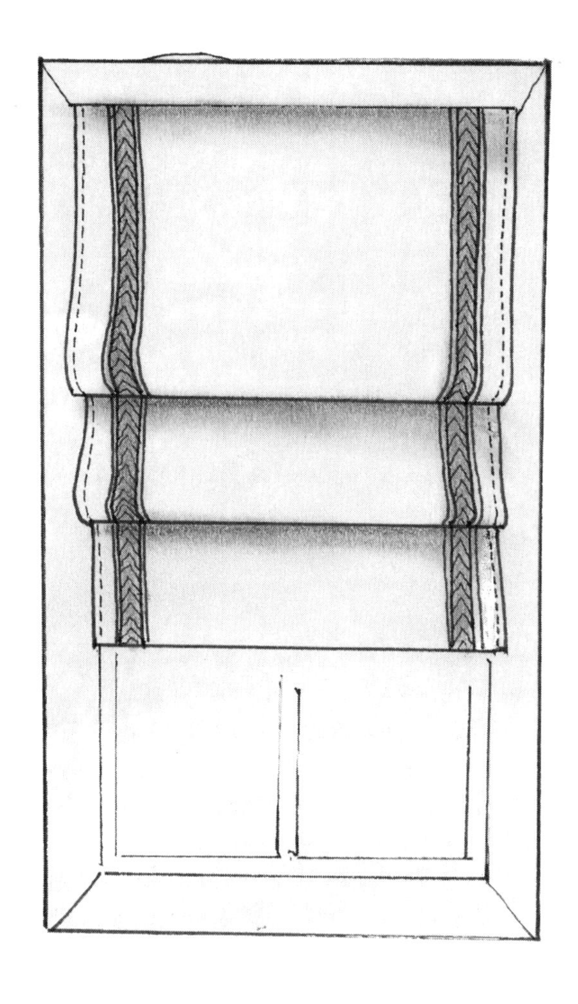

3

4

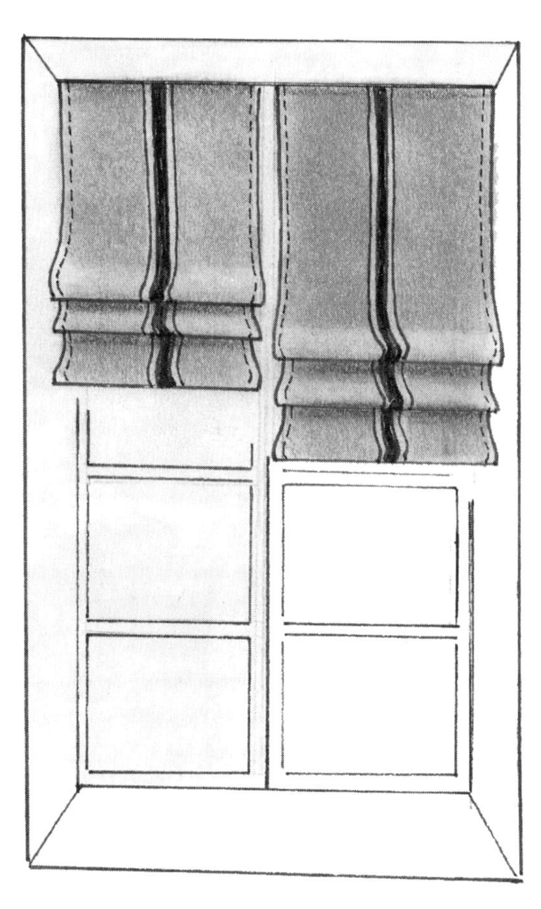

5

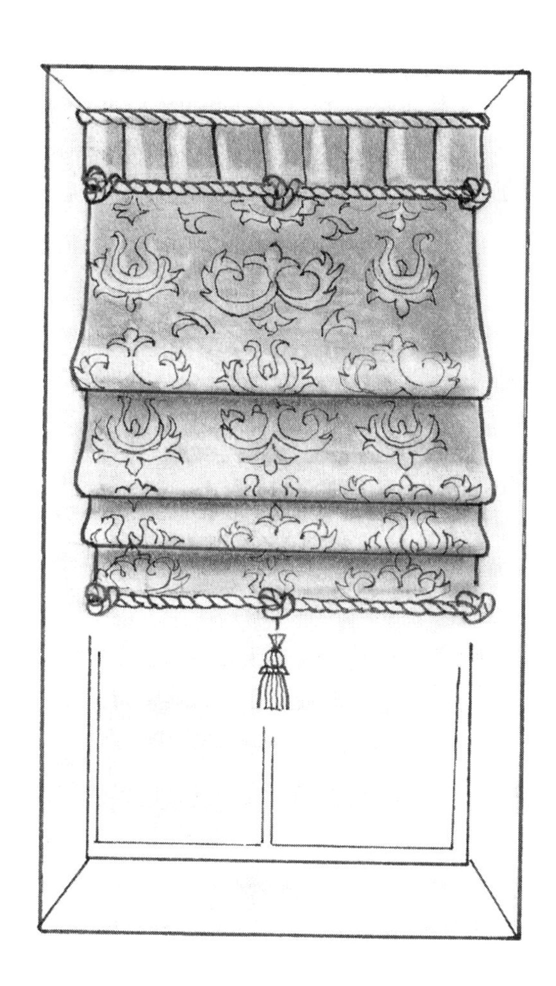

6

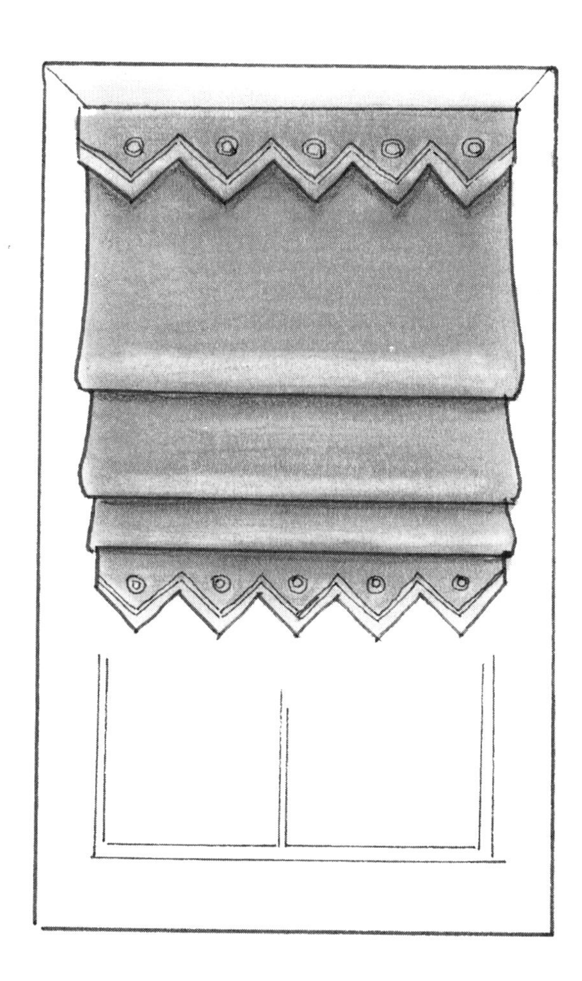

7

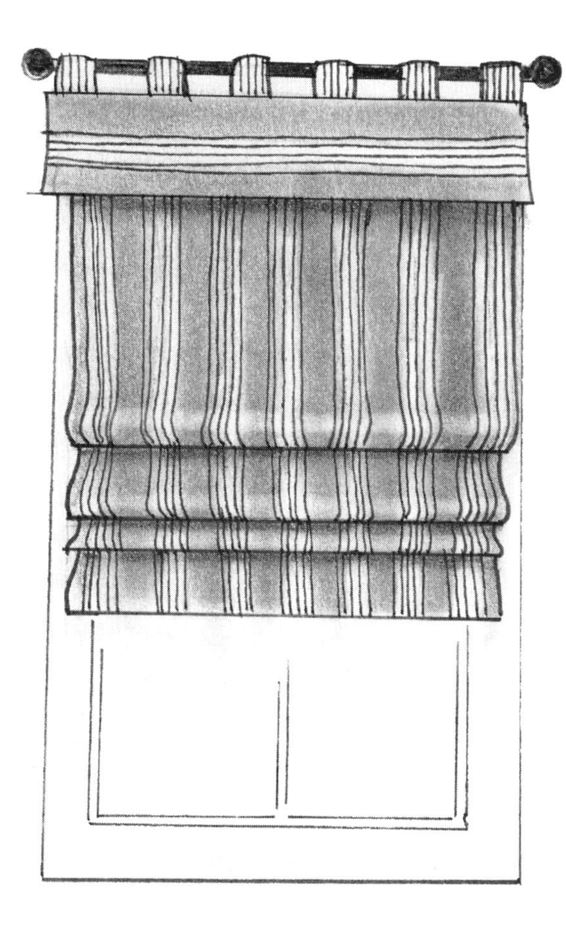

8

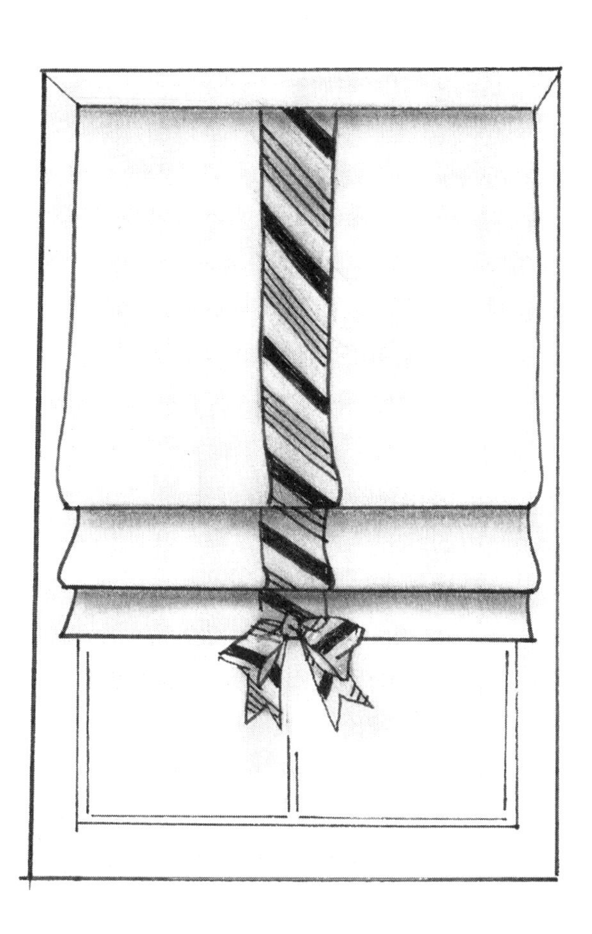

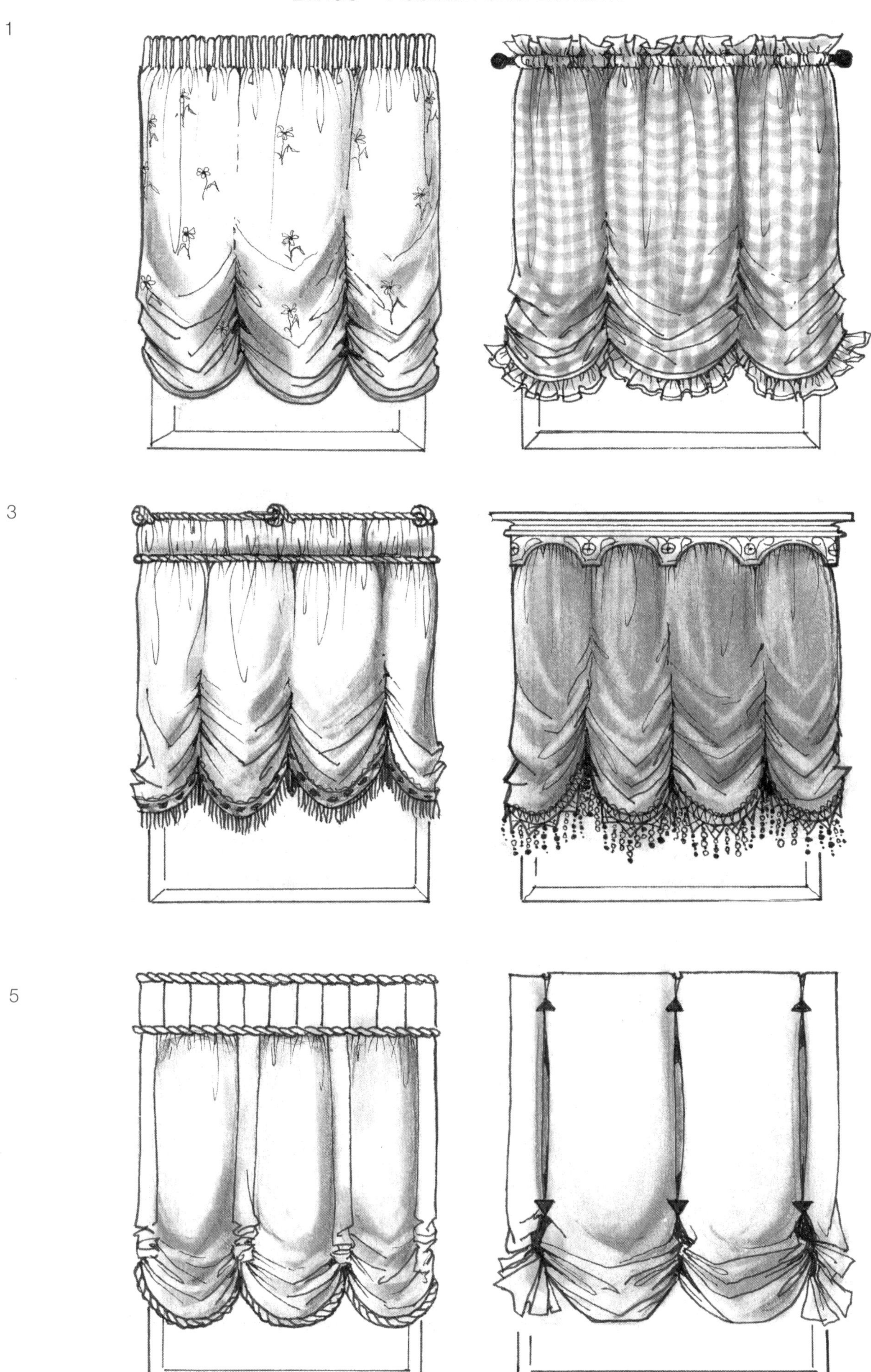
1
2
3
4
5
6

7

8

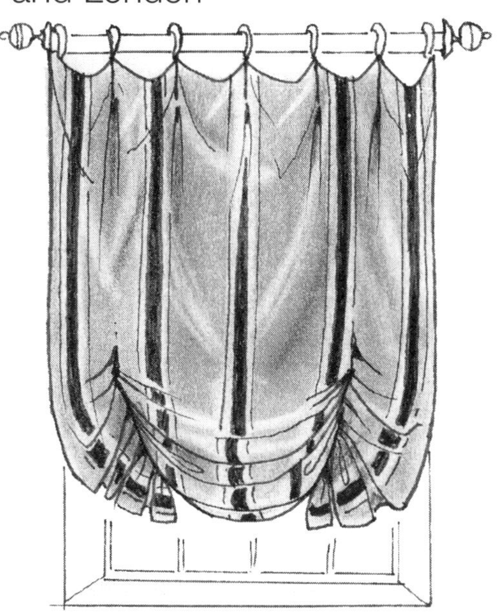

9

10

11

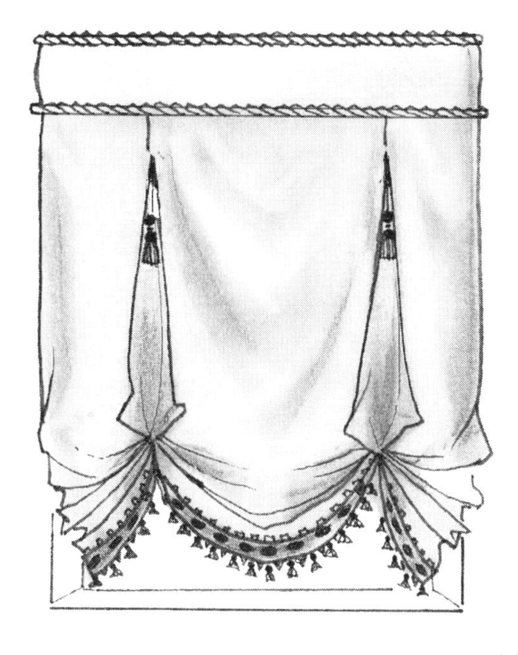

12

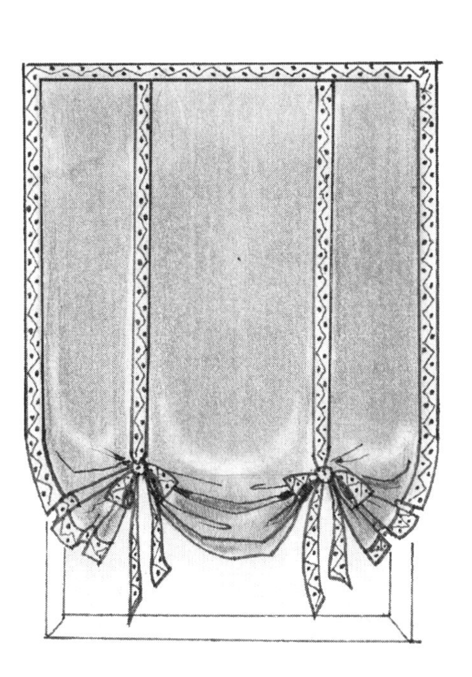

Table Covers

1

2

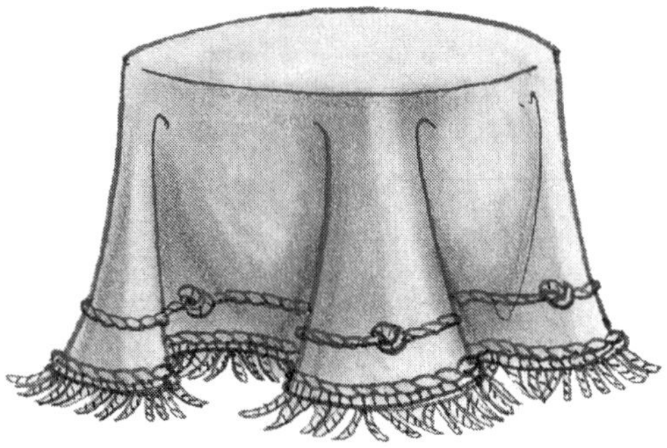

3

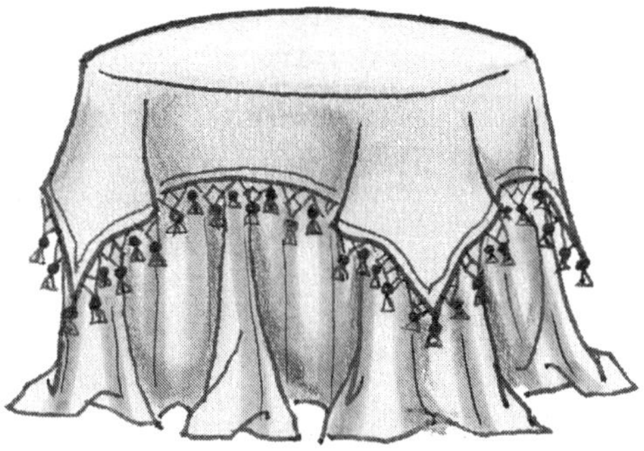

4

5

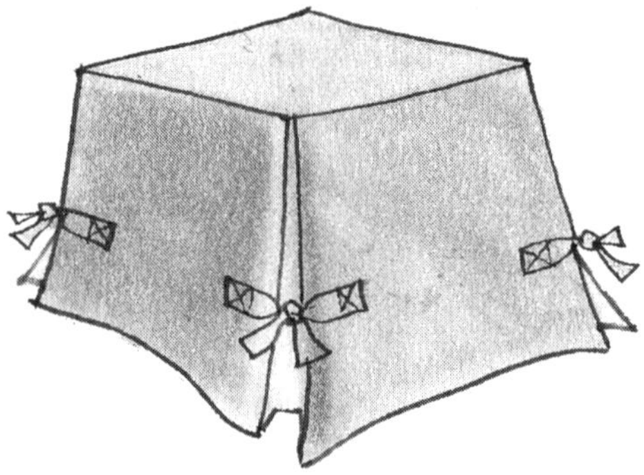

6

7

8

9

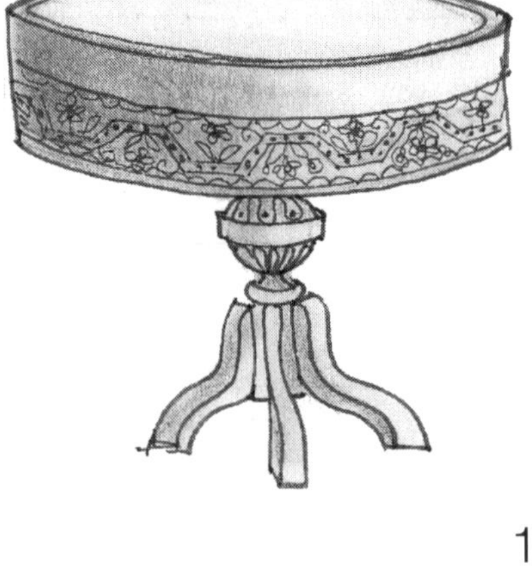

10

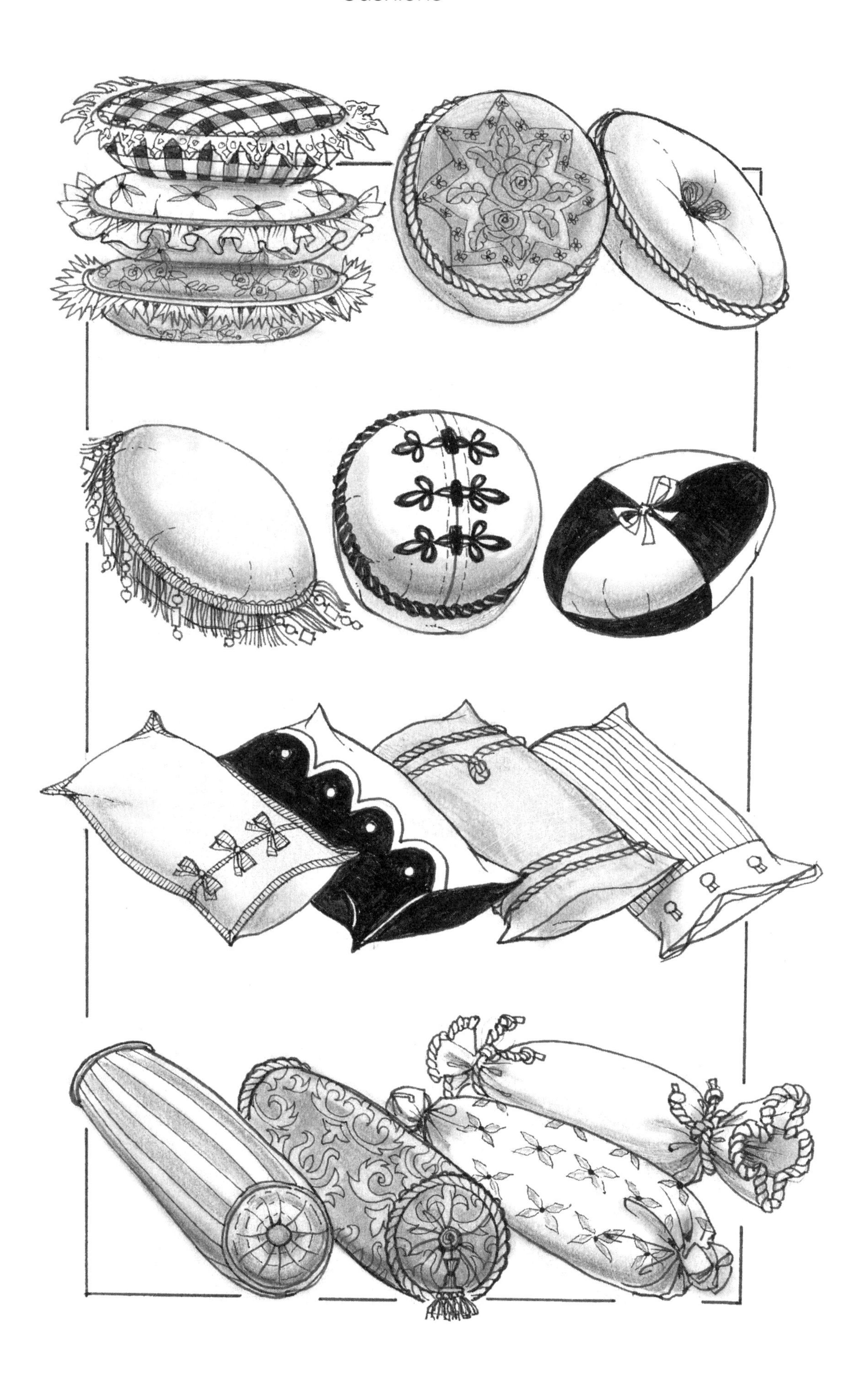

Platinum Range

All our Sateens have traceable yarns and are woven only in approved mills
The Platinum is our superior range with a construction of 72 x116 30s/30s

Product Code	Fibre Composition	Width	Colours
6202	100% Cotton Sateen	137cm	Ivory & Cream
6201	100% Cotton Sateen	137cm	Ivory & Cream
6203	100% Cotton Sateen	137cm	White, Ivory & Cream
6204	100% Cotton Sateen	137cm	Ivory & Cream

Chromax Range

This is our Premium Lining Range with many options to suit all types of fabrics and make up.

Product Code	Fibre Composition	Width	Colours
6851	100% Cotton Sateen	137cm	White, Ivory, Cream, Beige & Pale Ivory
6101	100% Cotton Sateen	137cm	White, Ivory, Cream, Beige & Black
6216	100% Cotton Sateen	137cm	Ivory & Cream
4936	100% Cotton Sateen	122cm	Ivory & Cream
6842	100% Cotton Sateen	300cm	Ivory
6800	100% Cotton Sateen	137cm	66 colours
6803	100% Cotton Chintz	137cm	29 colours

Eurolining

For use with poly/cotton face fabrics or for reasons of minimal shrinkage, crease resistance and easy care, poly cottons are an ideal choice

Product Code	Fibre Composition	Width	Colours
6502	50% Poly 50% Cotton	137cm	Ivory & Cream
6506	50% Poly 50% Cotton	142cm	White, Ivory & Cream
6511	50% Poly 50% Cotton	284cm	Ivory & Cream
6209	70% Poly 30% Cotton.	137cm	Ivory
6226	70% Poly 30% Cotton.	150cm	Ivory
6520	70% Poly 30% Cotton.	274cm	Ivory
6513	50% Poly 50% Cotton	137cm	Ivory
6518	50% Poly 50% Cotton	173cm	Ivory
6519	50% Poly 50% Cotton	244cm	Ivory
6514	50% Poly 50% Cotton	274cm	Ivory

Elements

Our Elements Blackout Linings are performance fabrics produced to increase thermal insulation properties of curtains, thus conserving energy, and providing a blackout measure, for example to childrens or night workers bedrooms. All thermal and blackout coatings have passed rigorous UV accelerated weathering tests with no degeneration of the acrylic coating

Product Code	Fibre Composition	Width	Colours
6968	Super soft 3 pass 50% Poly 50% Cotton	137cm	White & Cream
6971	Super soft 3 pass 50% Poly 50% Cotton	274cm	White & Cream
6319	3 pass 70% Poly 30% Cotton.	137cm	White/White & White/Ivory
6324	Super soft Thermal 50% Poly 50% Cotton	137cm	Beige
6323	Super soft Thermal 50% Poly 50% Cotton	274cm	White & Beige

Intermax

Interlining are the essential component in your curtains, bringing ultimate luxury, drape and improved appearance. They provide acoustic thermal properties, ensuring a cool room in summer and a warm room for those winter months

Product Code	Fibre Composition	Width	Colours
6402	64% Polyester 34% Viscose Stitch web	137cm	White
6401	64% Polyester 34% Viscose Stitch web	137cm	White
6403	64% Polyester 34% Viscose	150cm	White
6434	100% Polyester Stitch Web	137cm	White
6442	70% Polyester 30% Viscose Stitch Web	140cm	White
6414	76% Cotton,21%Viscose, 3% Polyamide	137cm	Natural
6441	70% Cotton 30% Polyester	150cm	Natural
6480	100% Polyester Stitch Web	280cm	White
6194	65% Cotton 35% Other fibres Bump	137cm	Bleached
6195	65% Cotton 35% Other fibres Bump	137cm	Natural
6191	65% Cotton 35% Other fibres Bump	137cm	Natural
6277	100% Cotton Twill Domette	137cm	Bleached
6256	100% Cotton Twill Domette	137cm	Natural
6426	100% Cotton Twill	137cm	Bleached
6244	100% Cotton Twill	137cm	Natural
6440	Pre Shrunk 100% Cotton	137cm	Bleached
6438	Pre Shrunk 100% Cotton	137cm	Natural

Duoline

This bonded lining to interling offers considerable savings in both cost and time.

Product Code	Fibre Composition	Width	Colours
6407	Cotton Sateen with wadding backing	137cm	Cream & Pale Ivory
6408	Poly/Cotton with Fleece backing	137cm	Ivory
6418	Cotton Sateen with Fleece backing	137cm	Ivory
6450	Chromax Colours with Fleece backing	137cm	9 colours
6420	Blackout with Fleece backing	137cm	White & Ivory

These are just a few of the many options we stock and we also have other alternatives like Flame Retardant products and Face fabrics

Please phone Edmund Bell for more information regarding products & prices on 01274680680

Notes

Notes

Edmund Bell

Notes

Notes

Edmund Bell

Notes

Notes

Notes

Edmund Bell

Notes